MIC 8/06

PA
02/10

mc

HOME PLATE DON'T MOVE

D1115515

DISCARDED

Bruce County Public Library
1243 Mackenzie Rd.
Port Elgin ON N0H 2C6

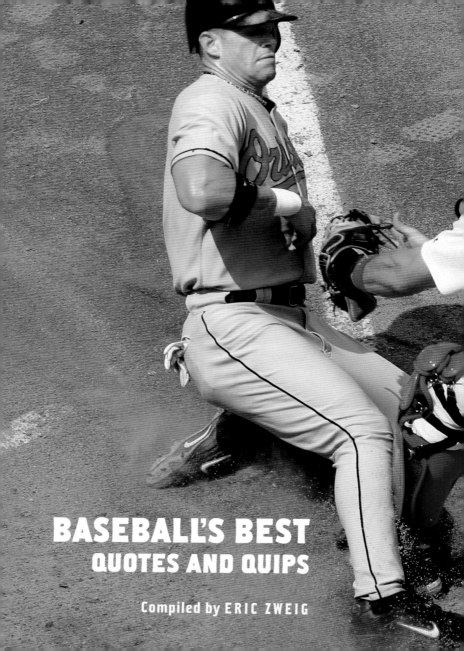

BASEBALL'S BEST
QUOTES AND QUIPS

Compiled by ERIC ZWEIG

HOME PLATE DON'T MOVE

Firefly Books

A FIREFLY BOOK

Published by Firefly Books Ltd. 2006

Copyright © 2006 Eric Zweig

All rights reserved. No part of this publication may be reproduced, stored in a retrieval system, or transmitted in any form or by any means, electronic, mechanical, photocopying, recording or otherwise, without the prior written permission of the Publisher.

First printing

PUBLISHER CATALOGING-IN-PUBLICATION DATA (U.S.)
Home plate don't move : baseball's best quotes and quips / compiled by Eric Zweig.
[176] p. ; photos (chiefly col.) :   cm.
Includes index.
ISBN-13: 978-1-55407-141-8
ISBN-10: 1-55407-141-0 (pbk.)
1. Baseball — Quotations, maxims, etc. I. Zweig, Eric, 1963-
II. Title.
793.357 dc22   GV873.3H66 2006

LIBRARY AND ARCHIVES CANADA CATALOGUING IN PUBLICATION
Zweig, Eric, 1963-
Home plate don't move : baseball's best quotes and quips / compiled by Eric Zweig.
Includes index.
ISBN-13: 978-1-55407-141-8
ISBN-10: 1-55407-141-0
1. Baseball—Quotations, maxims, etc.   I. Title.
GV873.Z94 2006   793357   C2005-905879-X

Published in the United States by
Firefly Books (U.S.) Inc.
P.O. Box 1338, Ellicott Station
Buffalo, New York 14205

Published in Canada by
Firefly Books Ltd.
66 Leek Crescent
Richmond Hill, Ontario L4B 1H1

Cover and interior design by Sari Naworynski
Printed in China

The publisher gratefully acknowledges the financial support for our publishing program by the Canada Council for the Arts, the Ontario Arts Council and the Government of Canada through the Book Publishing Industry Development Program.

For my mother, the reason we're fans.
For my brothers, who make it more fun.
For Barbara and Amanda, because they do, too.
And for my father, who would have liked this.

CONTENTS

INTRODUCTION

I can remember a reporter asking for a quote, and I didn't know what a quote was. I thought it was some kind of soft drink.

Joe DiMaggio, on life as a 20-year-old rookie in 1936

Yes, it's true. There was once a time when professional athletes were not so media savvy. And it was a lot more recently than when Joe DiMaggio was breaking in with the New York Yankees 70 years ago. When I was first watching baseball in the late 1970s and early 1980s, there was no ESPN, no all-sports radio and no Internet. We watched "The Game of the Week" on Saturday afternoons and were happy to get the occasional local broadcast. Mel Allen gave us our seven-day allotment of out-of-town highlights on "This Week in Baseball." Otherwise, we read about it in the newspapers, or heard about it on the radio ... just like the fans in DiMaggio's day.

The Yankee Clipper was a can't-miss superstar while he was still in his teens. At age 19 in 1935, when he was with the San Francisco Seals, DiMaggio earned MVP honors with a .398 average, 270 hits, 456 total bases, 34 homers, 48 doubles, 18 triples, 173 RBIs and 24 stolen bases in 25 attempts. With numbers like these, it's hard to believe we wouldn't see him interviewed a time or two on a cable sports channel. If DiMaggio were a rookie today, he'd arrive in the Majors fully prepared to deal with the media onslaught.

Of course, Joe DiMaggio was probably exaggerating his lack of sophistication. (Though judging by the pictures of him as a youngster, perhaps not!) Long before the 1930s, baseball was already filled with colorful characters who were quick with a quip, and sportswriters who were willing to immortalize them.

So what is it about baseball that lends itself to remarkable writing and clever quotes? Author W.P. Kinsella thinks it has something to do with the fact that in baseball, the ball is actually only in play for about five minutes out of three hours. "This makes baseball a game of anticipation; a game for the thinking fan, a game where little gems of wisdom or whimsy can be created in the dugout, the bullpen or the press box during long, hot afternoons and evenings of baseball."

This book is a celebration of those little gems of wisdom or whimsy, whether they come about as Kinsella says, or as a result of the complaint Los Angeles Dodgers slugger Pedro Guerrero once made about those who sit up in the press box. "Sometimes they write what I say," he lamented, "and not what I mean."

More than 400 quotations appear on the pages that follow, arranged by topic. Some are as timely as today's headlines, while many others are timeless. There should be something for everyone who likes insight, insults or inanity. As Babe Ruth once said, "The only real game, I think, is baseball." So whether you grew up watching Joe DiMaggio, Reggie Jackson or Derek Jeter (or Dizzy Dean, Don Drysdale or Pedro Martinez if you prefer pitching and hate the Yankees), I think you'll have fun flipping through these pages. After all, as San Francisco Giants pitcher Tyler Walker pointed out when an injury to Armando Benitez forced him into the closer's role early in the 2005 season, "You have to believe in your stuff ... and be convicted to each pitch."

Enjoy!

"You gotta be a man to play baseball for a living, but you gotta have a lot of little boy in you, too."

BROOKLYN DODGERS HALL OF FAME CATCHER
ROY CAMPANELLA

"Doctors tell me I have the body of a 30-year-old. I know I have the brain of a 15-year-old. If you've got both, you can play baseball."

CINCINNATI RED PETE ROSE, BACK WITH THE TEAM
AT AGE 44 IN 1985

"He looks like he's 15, plays like he's 25 and has the maturity of a man of 30."

MINNESOTA TWINS MANAGER GENE MAUCH,
ON 20-YEAR-OLD ROOKIE CATCHER BUTCH WYNEGAR,
THE FOURTH-YOUNGEST PLAYER IN THE MAJORS IN 1976

"When you're 21, you're a prospect. When you're 30, you're a suspect."

CHICAGO WHITE SOX PITCHER JIM MCGLOTHIN

"Age is a question of mind over matter. If you don't mind, it doesn't matter."

NEGRO LEAGUE SUPERSTAR SATCHEL PAIGE, WHOSE TRUE
AGE WAS UNKNOWN, BUT WHO WAS THOUGHT TO BE 42
WHEN HE MADE HIS MAJOR LEAGUE DEBUT IN 1948

"Every time I sign a ball, and there must have been thousands, I thank my luck that I wasn't born Coveleski, or Wambsganss or Peckinpaugh."

NEW YORK GIANTS HALL OF FAMER MEL OTT

"When I was a little kid, teachers used to punish me by making me sign my name 100 times."

KANSAS CITY ROYAL WILLIE WILSON ON WHY HE REFUSED TO SIGN AUTOGRAPHS

"Any **ballplayer** that don't sign autographs for little kids ain't an **American**. He's a **communist**."

RETIRED HALL OF FAMER ROGERS HORNSBY IN 1963

"Everybody in the park knows he's going to run, and he makes it anyway."

PHILADELPHIA PHILLY LARRY BOWA ON ST. LOUIS
CARDINAL LOU BROCK

"How can anyone as slow as you pull a muscle?"

CINCINNATI RED PETE ROSE TO HIS TEAMMATE
TONY PEREZ

"A good base stealer should make the whole infield jumpy. Whether you steal or not, you're changing the rhythm of the game. If the pitcher is concerned about you, he isn't concentrating enough on the batter."

HALL OF FAME SPEEDSTER-TURNED-BROADCASTER
JOE MORGAN

"He looks like a greyhound, but he runs like a bus."

KANSAS CITY ROYAL GEORGE BRETT, ON TEAMMATE
JAMIE QUIRK

"If my uniform doesn't get dirty, I haven't done anything in the baseball game."

ALL-TIME STOLEN BASE LEADER RICKEY HENDERSON,
WHILE IN HIS PRIME WITH THE OAKLAND A'S

"Baseball is the only field of endeavor where a man can succeed three times out of ten and be considered a good performer."

BOSTON RED SOX HALL OF FAMER **TED WILLIAMS**
(THE LAST MAN TO HIT .400)

"Trying to sneak a pitch past Hank Aaron is like trying to sneak the sunrise past a rooster."

MILWAUKEE BRAVES TEAMMATE **JOE ADCOCK**

"There have been only two geniuses in the world: Willie Mays and Willie Shakespeare."

ACTRESS AND BASEBALL FAN **TALLULAH BANKHEAD**

"He's got power enough to hit home runs in any park, including Yellowstone."

CINCINNATI REDS MANAGER **SPARKY ANDERSON,**
ON PITTSBURGH PIRATES SLUGGER WILLIE STARGELL

"He could hit .300 with a fountain pen."

ST. LOUIS CARDINAL **JOE GARAGIOLA** ON TEAMMATE AND
HALL OF FAMER STAN MUSIAL

"I might be shy, but in the field, where I have to do my work, I do it. I let my bat speak for myself."

LOS ANGELES ANGEL AND 2004 AMERICAN LEAGUE MVP VLADIMIR GUERRERO

"I believe he's been reincarnated, that he played before, in the 20s and 30s, and he's back to prove something."

FORMER ST. LOUIS CARDINALS TEAMMATE MARK MCGWIRE, ON ALBERT PUJOLS

"George Brett could roll out of bed on Christmas morning and hit a line drive."

KANSAS CITY ROYALS GM JOHN SCHUERHOLTZ

"He once hit a ball between my legs so hard that my center fielder caught it on the fly backing up against the wall."

ST. LOUIS CARDINALS GREAT DIZZY DEAN, ON FELLOW HALL OF FAMER BILL TERRY OF THE NEW YORK GIANTS

"My own little rule was two for one. If one of my
teammates got knocked down, then I knocked
down two on the other team."

LOS ANGELES DODGER DON DRYSDALE

"I heard he could hit."

ST. LOUIS CARDINAL BOB GIBSON'S REPLY TO HANK
AARON, WHEN ASKED WHY HE BEANED JOHN MILNER

"I'll tell you what, if he hit a home run off Gibson or
Drysdale and stood and admired it, they'd knock
that earring out of his ear the next time up."

NATIONAL LEAGUE UMPIRE DOUG HARVEY
ON BARRY BONDS

"It's always the same; Combs walks, Koening singles,
Ruth hits one out of the park, Gehrig doubles, Lazzeri
triples. Then Dugan goes in the dirt on his can."

NEW YORK YANKEE JOE DUGAN, ON BATTING IN THE
TEAM'S "MURDERERS ROW" LINEUP OF THE 1920S

"I hated to bat against Drysdale. After he hit you
he'd come around, look at the bruise on your arm
and say, 'Do you want me to sign it?'"

NEW YORK YANKEES LEGEND MICKEY MANTLE

"If you don't think baseball is a big deal, don't do it. But if you do it, do it right."

NEW YORK METS HALL OF FAME PITCHER **TOM SEAVER**

"I'm a ballplayer, not an actor."

NEW YORK YANKEES LEGEND **JOE DIMAGGIO**, ON WHY HE
ALWAYS LOOKED SO SERIOUS

"I never smile when I have a bat in my hands. That's when you've got to be serious. When I get out in the field, nothing's a joke to me. I don't feel I should walk around with a smile on my face."

MILWAUKEE BRAVE **HANK AARON**, BASEBALL'S ALL-TIME
HOME RUN LEADER, AS A YOUNG PLAYER IN 1956

"If somebody came up and hit .450, stole 100 bases and performed a miracle in the field every day, I'd still look you in the eye and say Willie Mays was better."

LEO DUROCHER, WHO MANAGED WILLIE MAYS IN HIS EARLY DAYS WITH THE NEW YORK GIANTS

"The fans don't see it, because we make it look so efficient, but internally, for a guy to be successful, you have to be like a clock spring – wound but loose at the same time."

NEW YORK YANKEE **DAVE WINFIELD**

"The severity of injuries on a pain scale doesn't compare in baseball and hockey. If you talked to a hockey player about having a bone spur or a bone chip, he'd laugh."

CANADIAN-BORN PITCHER **KIRK MCCASKILL**, WHO WAS AN ALL-AMERICAN HOCKEY PLAYER AT THE UNIVERSITY OF VERMONT

"Like I say, it's almost embarrassing to talk about. I don't know if Michael Jordan or Bill Gates or Alexander the Great or anyone is worth this type of money, but that's the market we're in today. That's what Mr. Hicks decided to pay me, and now it's time to pay him back and win a couple championships."

ALEX RODRIGUEZ, AFTER SIGNING HIS 10-YEAR, $250-MILLION CONTRACT WITH THE TEXAS RANGERS

"What happens is that all your life you operated businesses in such a way that you could one day afford to buy a baseball team. And then you buy the team and forget all the business practices that enabled you to buy it."

NEW YORK YANKEES OWNER GEORGE STEINBRENNER

"The bigger the contract, the bigger the responsibility."

PEDRO MARTINEZ, ON SIGNING A DEAL WORTH $53 MILLION OVER FOUR YEARS WITH THE NEW YORK METS AFTER THE 2004 SEASON

"There was a time when the National League stood for integrity and fair dealing. Today it stands for dollars and cents. Once it looked to the elevation of the game and an honest exhibition of the sport; today its eyes are on the turnstile... Players have been bought, sold and exchanged as though they were sheep instead of American citizens."

HALL OF FAMER JOHN MONTGOMERY WARD, WHO ORGANIZED A PLAYERS UNION IN 1890

"Baseball has prostituted itself. Pretty soon we'll be starting games at midnight so the people in outer space can watch on prime time. We're making a mistake by always going for more money."

SAN DIEGO PADRES OWNER RAY KROC, ON TELEVISION'S CONTROL OF BASEBALL IN 1977

"If I were sitting down with George Steinbrenner ... I'd have to say, 'George, you and I are about to become partners.'"

NEW YORK YANKEES LEGEND JOE DIMAGGIO, WHOSE $100,000 SALARY IN 1951 WAS THEN THE BIGGEST IN BASEBALL HISTORY, ON WHAT HE'D HAVE BEEN WORTH IN THE FREE AGENT ERA

"They know when to cheer and they know when to boo. And they know when to drink beer. They do it all the time."

BREWERS SLUGGER **GORMAN THOMAS** ON THE FANS IN MILWAUKEE

"You're trying your damndest, you strike out and they boo you. I act like it doesn't bother me, like I don't hear anything the fans say, but the truth is I hear every word of it and it kills me."

PHILLIES HALL OF FAMER **MIKE SCHMIDT** ON THE FANS IN PHILADELPHIA

"I don't care who you are, you hear those boos."

NEW YORK YANKEES LEGEND **MICKEY MANTLE**

"I've never heard a crowd boo a homer, but I've heard plenty of boos after a strike out."

NEW YORK YANKEES IMMORTAL **BABE RUTH**

"Rooting for the Yankees is like rooting for U.S. Steel."

COMIC **JOE E. LEWIS**

"Breaks like a ball falling off a pool table."

LEGENDARY MANAGER **LEO DUROCHER** ON THE FLIGHT OF
A GOOD CURVEBALL

"His curveball, it jelly-legs you."

CLEVELAND INDIAN **JIM THOME**, ON OAKLAND A'S PITCHER
BARRY ZITO

"The secret to all of them is they're thrown so hard.
That's what makes his slider, or Carlton's or mine
different from all the other ones. Because we throw
hard, it looks like a fastball."

NEW YORK YANKEES GREAT **RON GUIDRY** ON THE SLIDERS
THROWN BY HIM, STEVE CARLTON AND RANDY JOHNSON

"Hitters always have one thing in mind – they have
to protect themselves against the fastball. If they're
not ready for the fastball, a pitcher will throw it right
by them. If they're ready for the fastball and don't
get it, they can adjust to the breaking ball. But with
a screwball, it isn't the break that fools the hitter,
it's the change of speed. They don't time it."

NEW YORK GIANTS HALL OF FAME PITCHER **CARL HUBBELL**,
WHOSE MAIN PITCH WAS THE SCREWBALL

"It is a grueling position. My knees will tell you that. I've had nine knee surgeries. I've had a couple of broken thumbs, one on each hand. I can look back at it and say it's worth it to be enshrined in Cooperstown. I don't have any pain in my knees right now."

GARY CARTER, ON BECOMING ONE OF ONLY 14 CATCHERS IN THE BASEBALL HALL OF FAME

"Catching is much like managing. Managers don't really win games, but they can lose plenty of them. The same way with catching."

PHILADELPHIA PHILLY **BOB BOONE**, WHO CAUGHT MORE MAJOR LEAGUE GAMES THAN ANYONE IN BASEBALL HISTORY

"A good catcher is the quarterback, the carburetor, the lead dog, the pulse taker, the traffic cop and sometimes a lot of unprintable things, but no team gets very far without one."

NEW YORK YANKEES HALL OF FAME MANAGER **MILLER HUGGINS**

"That isn't an arm, that's a rifle."

FELLOW CATCHER **GENE TENACE** OF THE OAKLAND A'S AFTER SEEING JOHNNY BENCH THROW TO SECOND BASE

"I don't recall the name, but you sure were a sucker for a high curve inside."

NEW YORK YANKEES HALL OF FAME CATCHER **BILL DICKEY**, TO A FORMER PLAYER WHO CAME UP TO HIM AND ASKED IF HE REMEMBERED HIM

"By the end of the season, I feel like a used car."

SAN FRANCISCO GIANTS CATCHER **BOB BRENLY**

"I don't want them to forget Ruth. I just want them to remember me."

ATLANTA BRAVES HALL OF FAMER HANK AARON, AS HE CLOSED IN ON BABE RUTH'S RECORD OF 714 HOME RUNS LATE IN 1973

"They just say they'll be disappointed if anyone tops Babe Ruth. But if I do, I expect someone to top me someday."

HANK AARON, WHO'S RECORD IS STILL STANDING THROUGH THE 2005 SEASON

"Maybe I'm not a great man, but I damn well want to break the record."

NEW YORK YANKEE ROGER MARIS, ON CHASING RUTH'S SINGLE SEASON RECORD OF 60 HOME RUNS LATE IN 1961

"As a ballplayer, I would be delighted to do it again. As an individual, I doubt if I could possibly go through it again."

ROGER MARIS, ON HITTING 61 HOMERS IN 1961

"It's the most overused word in baseball. When my teams have gone well, it has been said I'm a good communicator. When they have gone bad, it has been said I've lost the ability to communicate. But the truth is, through all of it, I have been my same obnoxious self."

SAN DIEGO PADRES MANAGER **DICK WILLIAMS**

"When you're winning, they say you have aggressive players when they spout off. When you're losing, they call it dissension."

VETERAN PLAYER AND MANAGER **HARRY WALKER**

"Dissension? We got no dissension. What we ain't got is pitchers."

BROOKLYN DODGERS CATCHER **ROY CAMPANELLA**, DURING A TEAM SLUMP IN 1950

"There are two things about them. If you don't have any, it's bad. If you have too many, it's worse."

SAN FRANCISCO GIANTS MANAGER **FELIPE ALOU**, ON THE VALUE OF TEAM MEETINGS

"My father is 85 years old. He says the last time the Cubs were in the World Series he had tickets, but General George Patton wouldn't let him go. He had to go fight World War II."

LONG-TIME CHICAGO CUBS FAN **HARVEY BROWN**, QUOTED IN A NEW YORK TIMES ARTICLE AFTER BOSTON WON THE WORLD SERIES IN 2004 FOR THE FIRST TIME SINCE 1918. (THE CUBS HAVE NOT WON SINCE 1908, AND HAVE NOT EVEN PLAYED IN THE WORLD SERIES SINCE 1945.)

"Things were so bad in Chicago last summer that by the fifth inning we were selling hot dogs to go."

CHICAGO WHITE SOX PITCHER **KEN BRETT**

"If I was going to storm a pillbox, going to sheer, utter, certain death, and the colonel said, 'Shepherd, pick six guys,' I'd pick six White Sox fans, because they have known death every day of their lives and it holds no terror for them."

HUMORIST **JEAN SHEPHERD**

"Chicago, Second City no more."

FIRST BASEMAN **PAUL KONERKO** AFTER THE WHITE SOX ENDED AN 88-YEAR WORLD SERIES DROUGHT IN 2005

"George Hendrick simply lost that sun-blown pop-up."

**HALL OF FAME BROADCASTER (AND EX-BALLPLAYER)
JERRY COLEMAN**

"He slides into second with a stand-up double."

JERRY COLEMAN

"It's a cold night out tonight. The Padres better warm up real good because it's stiff out there."

JERRY COLEMAN

"Rich Folkers is throwing up in the bullpen."

JERRY COLEMAN

"There's a fly ball to center field. Winfield is going back, back... He hits his head against the wall... It's rolling towards second base..."

JERRY COLEMAN

"Unless I'm mistaken, we've won four straight before."

RED SOX CENTER FIELDER **JOHNNY DAMON**, COMMENTING ON BOSTON'S CHANCES AFTER LOSING THE FIRST THREE GAMES OF THE 2004 AMERICAN LEAGUE CHAMPIONSHIP SERIES TO THE RIVAL NEW YORK YANKEES. BOSTON BECAME THE FIRST TEAM IN BASEBALL HISTORY TO BOUNCE BACK FROM A THREE-GAMES-TO-NOTHING DEFICIT, AND THEN WENT ON TO WIN THE WORLD SERIES FOR THE FIRST TIME SINCE 1918

"The death toll in New England will be catastrophic. There are so many old people saying, 'I can't die until I see them win the World Series.' They are all going to die. It's going to be worse than the Black Plague."

BOSTON RED SOX FAN **PAUL SULLIVAN**, ON THE DOWNSIDE OF BOSTON WINNING THE 2004 WORLD SERIES

"When people thank you for doing something, you begin to realize how truly blessed you were to have been put in that position."

BOSTON RED SOX CATCHER **JASON VARITEK** ON HIS REACTION TO THE BEHAVIOR OF RED SOX FANS DURING THE WINTER AFTER THEIR 2004 WORLD SERIES VICTORY

"So, like, what took you so long?"

PRESIDENT **GEORGE W. BUSH**, GREETING THE RED SOX AT THE WHITE HOUSE IN 2004

"When he punched Keith Hernandez in spring training last season, it was the only time that Strawberry would hit the cut-off man all year."

SPORTSWRITER STEVE WULF, ON NEW YORK DARRYL STRAWBERRY

"They should've called a welder."

FORMER GOLD GLOVE OUTFIELDER RICHIE ASHBURN, THEN AN ANNOUNCER, WATCHING DAVE KINGMAN OF THE NEW YORK METS HAVE HIS GLOVE REPAIRED

"Because you're a .399 fielder."

ST. LOUIS CARDINALS MANAGER BILLY SOUTHWORK, EXPLAINING TO .400-HITTING ROOKIE DON PADGETT WHY HE WAS RIDING THE BENCH

"He plays the outfield like he's trying to catch grenades."

NEW YORK YANKEES SLUGGER REGGIE JACKSON – NO GOLD GLOVER HIMSELF – ON SPEEDSTER CLAUDELL WASHINGTON

"It's not that Reggie is a bad outfielder. He just has trouble judging the ball and picking it up."

NEW YORK YANKEES MANAGER BILLY MARTIN, ON REGGIE JACKSON

"They wanted me to play third base like Brooks, so I did play like Brooks – Mel Brooks."

OUTFIELDER **ANDY VAN SLYKE,** RECALLING HIS EARLY
DAYS AS A ST. LOUIS CARDINALS THIRD BASEMAN

"Me and Paul will probably win 40 games this year."

> **DIZZY DEAN'S** BOAST ABOUT HOW HE AND HIS BROTHER
> WOULD DO WITH THE ST. LOUIS CARDINALS IN 1934. HE WAS
> WRONG – THEY WON 49. (DIZZY WAS 30-7, WHILE PAUL WAS
> 19-11.)

"If I had known what Paul was gonna do, I would have pitched one too."

> **DIZZY DEAN,** AFTER HE PITCHED A ONE-HITTER IN THE
> FIRST GAME OF A DOUBLEHEADER AND BROTHER PAUL
> PITCHED A NO-HITTER IN THE SECOND

"Heck, if anybody told me I was setting a record I'd of got me some more strikeouts."

> **DIZZY DEAN,** ON HIS NATIONAL LEAGUE RECORD 17
> STRIKEOUTS ON JULY 30, 1933

"Son, what kind of a pitch would you like to miss?"

> WHAT **DIZZY DEAN** IS SAID TO HAVE ASKED A BATTER HE
> HAD STRUCK OUT ALL DAY

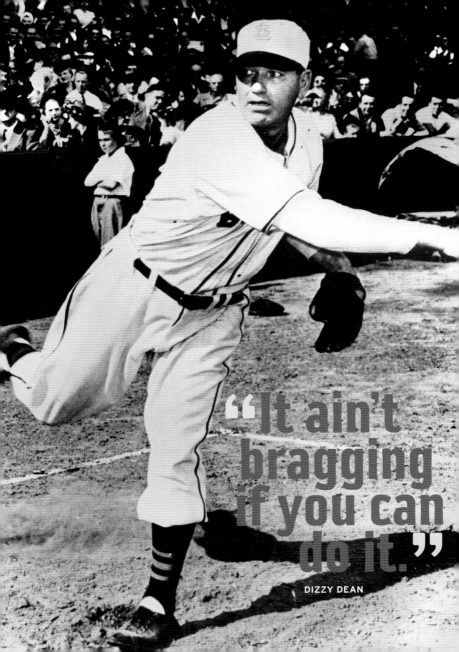

"It ain't bragging if you can do it."

DIZZY DEAN

"Sure, old Diz knows the King's English. And not only that, I also know the Queen is English."

DIZZY DEAN, IN RESPONSE TO A LISTENER'S CLAIM THAT HE DIDN'T KNOW "THE KING'S ENGLISH"

"The runners have returned to their respectable bases."

A STANDARD DIZZY DEAN LINE

"Ted Kluszewski was on third. Somebody like Odrowski on second, maybe Timowtiz on first. Boy, I was sweatin', hopin' nobody'd get a hit and I wouldn't have to call all those names."

DIZZY DEAN, ON A TOUGH DAY IN THE BROADCAST BOOTH

"Well, Pee Wee, I've been watching him for four innings and I believe that's a baseball he's throwing."

DIZZY DEAN, TO FELLOW PLAYER-TURNED-BROADCASTER PEE WEE REESE, WHEN ASKED ABOUT A PITCHER AND SET UP WITH "HE'S DOING A GREAT JOB. WHAT WOULD YOU SAY HE'S BEEN THROWING OUT THERE?" DEAN TOLD THE STORY TO THE SPORTING NEWS IN 1970, COMPLAINING THAT PRESENT-DAY BASEBALL ANNOUNCERS WERE TOO STATISTICS-MINDED AND TOO DULL

"A hot dog at the ballpark is better than steak at the Ritz."

HUMPHREY BOGART

"I've seen him order everything on the menu except 'Thank you for dining with us.'"

ATLANTA BRAVE JERRY ROYSTER, ON THE APPETITE OF TEAMMATE DALE MURPHY

"Butch Huskey might be the most appropriately named person in baseball since Cliff Ditto managed the minor-league team in Walla Walla, Washington."

NEW YORK METS GENERAL MANAGER JOE MCILVAINE, ON HIS TEAM'S YOUNG 244-POUND OUTFIELDER

"Jeter is a six-tool player. I've never eaten with him so I can't tell you if he has good table manners, but I would imagine he has those, too."

TEXAS RANGERS MANAGER JOHNNY OATES ON DEREK JETER

"All I want out of life is that when I walk down the street, folks will say, 'There goes the greatest hitter who ever lived.'"

BOSTON RED SOX LEGEND **TED WILLIAMS**, WHO BATTED .344 WITH 512 HOMERS

"If I'd just tried for them dinky singles I could've batted around .600."

NEW YORK YANKEES LEGEND **BABE RUTH**, WHO HIT 714 HOME RUNS AND HAD A LIFETIME BATTING AVERAGE OF .342

"I wish he were still playing. I'd probably crack his head open to show him how valuable I was."

1986 MVP **ROGER CLEMENS** OF THE BOSTON RED SOX AFTER HANK AARON SAID PITCHERS SHOULD NOT BE ELIGIBLE TO WIN THE MOST VALUABLE PLAYER AWARD

"It's called talent. I just have it. I can't explain it. You either have it or you don't."

SAN FRANCISCO GIANT **BARRY BONDS**

"**The only reason I don't like playing in the World Series is I can't watch myself play.**

NEW YORK YANKEES SUPERSTAR **REGGIE JACKSON**

"If they worked as hard at their jobs as I do at mine, this country wouldn't have the inflation problem it has now."

MINNESOTA TWIN **MIKE MARSHALL**, WHO MADE A RECORD 106 RELIEF APPEARANCES WITH THE LOS ANGELES DODGERS IN 1974, ON BEING BOOED BY MINNESOTA FANS IN 1980

"I don't talk about it, but I know the numbers of some of the shortstops in there and mine are better."

CINCINNATI RED **BARRY LARKIN**, WHO RETIRED BEFORE THE 2005 SEASON AFTER 20 YEARS WITH THE TEAM, ADMITTING THAT HE BELIEVES HE SHOULD MAKE IT TO THE HALL OF FAME

"I'd like to be remembered. I'd like to think that someday two guys will be talking in a bar and one of them will say something like, 'Yeah, he's a good shortstop, but he's not as good as ole Ripken was.'"

BALTIMORE ORIOLES GREAT **CAL RIPKEN, JR.**

"They can say whatever they want to say, but it is going to be hard, my friend, to duplicate me."

SAMMY SOSA, AT TRAINING CAMP WITH THE BALTIMORE ORIOLES IN 2005, REACTING TO FORMER CHICAGO CUBS TEAMMATES WHO SAID THEY WOULDN'T MISS HIM

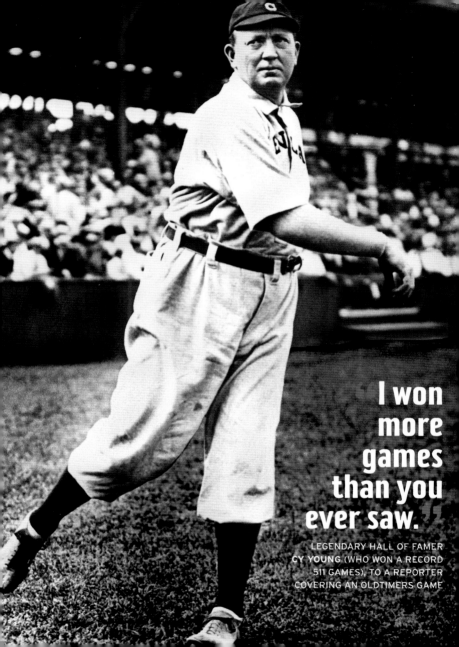

I won more games than you ever saw.

LEGENDARY HALL OF FAMER **CY YOUNG** (WHO WON A RECORD 511 GAMES), TO A REPORTER COVERING AN OLDTIMERS GAME

"Every hitter likes fastballs, just like everybody likes ice cream. But you don't like it when someone's stuffing it into you by the gallon."

NEW YORK YANKEE **REGGIE JACKSON**, ON FACING NOLAN RYAN, BASEBALL'S ALL-TIME STRIKEOUT LEADER WITH 5,714

"It starts out like a baseball, and when it gets to the plate it looks like a marble."

CHICAGO CUBS HALL OF FAMER **HACK WILSON**, ON SATCHEL PAIGE'S FASTBALL

"You can't hit what you can't see."

WASHINGTON SENATORS CATCHER **CLIFF BLANKENSHIP**, ON WHY HE HAD SIGNED FUTURE HALL OF FAME PITCHER WALTER JOHNSON WHILE SCOUTING FOR THE TEAM

"Hitters always have that fear that one pitch might get away from him, and they'll wind up DOA with a tag on their toe."

NEW YORK YANKEE **RUDY MAY**, ON THE FASTBALL OF YANKEES PITCHER GOOSE GOSSAGE

"When they operated, I told them to put in a Koufax fastball. They did – but it was Mrs. Koufax's."

LOS ANGELES DODGERS PITCHER **TOMMY JOHN**, REFERRING TO THE LIGAMENT TRANSPLANT OPERATION THAT NOW BEARS HIS NAME

"I'm getting by on three pitches now – a curve, a change-up, and whatever you want to call that thing that used to be my fastball."

DETROIT TIGERS FORMER FIREBALLER FRANK TANANA

"I'm throwing just as hard as I ever did. The ball's just not getting there as fast."

BOSTON RED SOX PITCHER **LEFTY GROVE**, A FUTURE HALL OF FAMER, ON THE PROBLEMS OF AGING

"One day I was pitching against Washington and the catcher called for a fastball. When it got to the plate, it was so slow that two pigeons were roosting on it. I decided to quit."

LONGTIME DETROIT TIGERS PITCHER **PAUL "DIZZY" TROUT**, ON HOW HE KNEW IT WAS TIME TO RETIRE

"First, it's just the gratification of knowing you hit the ball well. Then, you realize that you broke up a no-hitter and it's your first homer and it's off Pedro Martinez. When I got into the dugout, I really kind of had to sit down."

HOUSTON ASTROS ROOKIE **CHRIS BURKE**, WHOSE FIRST CAREER HOME RUN IN 2005 BROKE UP PEDRO MARTINEZ' BID TO TOSS THE FIRST NO-HITTER IN NEW YORK METS HISTORY

"I wanted to go into my home run trot, but then I realized I didn't have one."

WHITE SOX CATCHER **JIM ESSIAN**, ON HIS FIRST MAJOR LEAGUE HOMER

"Being on the mound for that first pitch, it was like I actually existed."

TORONTO BLUE JAYS PITCHER **DAVID BUSH**, ON MAKING HIS MAJOR LEAGUE DEBUT IN 2004

"Everyone who makes the big leagues has been a baseball standout all his life. Even so, from a big league viewpoint, he has everything to learn. It's unbelievable how much you don't know about the game you've been playing all your life."

NEW YORK YANKEES LEGEND **MICKEY MANTLE**

"To hit .400 you need a great start and you can't have a slump. The year I did it, I was around .410, .412 all season."

NEW YORK GIANT **BILLY TERRY**, WHO WAS THE LAST NATIONAL LEAGUE PLAYER TO HIT .400, BATTING .401 IN 1930

"It's July and, yeah, I'd be lying if I didn't say I want to make a crack at .400. But it's not going to be easy. It's going to be a lot more difficult than I think people think, but I just go out and play. I don't worry about the numbers."

SAN DIEGO PADRE **TONY GWYNN**, IN JULY OF 1997. HE HIT .372 THAT YEAR. (GWYNN HIT .394 IN THE STRIKE-SHORTENED SEASON OF 1994.)

"I hope somebody hits .400 soon. Then people can start pestering that guy."

TED WILLIAMS IN 1980. NO ONE HAS HIT .400 SINCE HE BATTED .406 FOR THE BOSTON RED SOX IN 1941

"It has been many years since anyone hit .400. I don't know if I'll ever do it. I just want to be a player people say has a chance."

SEATTLE MARINER **ICHIRO SUZUKI**, AT TRAINING CAMP IN 2005, AFTER BATTING .372 WITH A RECORD-SETTING 262 HITS IN 2004

"Ninety percent I'll spend on good times, women and Irish whiskey. The other ten percent I'll probably waste."

PHILADELPHIA PHILLIES RELIEVER **TUG MCGRAW**, ON HOW HE PLANNED TO SPEND HIS SALARY

"With the money I'm making, I should be playing
two positions."

PHILADELPHIA PHILLY **PETE ROSE**, AFTER SIGNING WITH
THE TEAM AS A FREE AGENT

"One year, I hit .291 and had to take a salary cut. If
you hit .291 today, you'd own the franchise."

RETIRED HALL OF FAMER **ENOS SLAUGHTER**

"I don't mind paying a player, but I don't want to
pay for his funeral."

TORONTO BLUE JAYS GM **PAT GILLICK**, ON THE DEMANDS
OF 39-YEAR-OLD RICO CARTY FOR A MULTIYEAR CONTRACT

"You keep the salary, I'll take the cut."

NEW YORK YANKEES HALL OF FAME PITCHER
VERNON (LEFTY) GOMEZ, TO TEAM OWNER COLONEL
JACOB RUPERT, WHEN HE THREATENED TO CUT HIS SALARY
FROM $20,000 TO $7,500 AFTER A BAD YEAR IN 1935

"I got a million dollars worth of free advice, and a
very small raise."

BROOKLYN DODGER **EDDIE STANKY**, ON NEGOTIATING WITH
BRANCH RICKEY

"Have one good year and you can fool them for five more, because for five more years they expect you to have another good one."

HALL OF FAME PLAYER AND MANAGER **FRANKIE FRISCH**

"It's easy to stay in the majors for seven-and-a-half years when you hit .300. But when you hit .216 like me, it's really an accomplishment."

CALIFORNIA ANGELS OUTFIELDER **JOE LAHOUD**

"It's not easy to hit .215. You have to be going terrible and have bad luck, too."

STRUGGLING PITTSBURGH PIRATES OUTFIELDER
STEVE KEMP

"The only mistake I made in my whole baseball career was hitting .361 that one year, because ever since then people have expected me to keep on doing it."

DETROIT TIGER AND 1961 AMERICAN LEAGUE BATTING
CHAMPION **NORM CASH**

"I'd rather have a **Gold Glove** than a **Silver Slugger**. Defense is so much more of a team game."

NEW YORK YANKEE **ALEX RODRIGUEZ**

"Don't get me wrong, I like to hit, but there's nothing like getting out there in the outfield, running after a ball and throwing somebody out trying to take that extra base. That's real fun."

NEW YORK/SAN FRANCISCO GIANTS HALL OF FAMER
WILLIE MAYS

"I can't very well tell my batters, 'Don't hit it to him.' Wherever they hit it, he's there anyway."

NEW YORK METS MANAGER GIL HODGES, ON WILLIE MAYS

"I don't know if it's my best catch ever, but it definitely came in the most important situation of my career."

TORONTO BLUE JAYS OUTFIELDER DEVON WHITE, ON THE
CATCH HE MADE IN GAME THREE OF THE 1992 WORLD
SERIES, WHICH ALMOST STARTED A TRIPLE PLAY AND HAS
BEEN COMPARED TO THE LEGENDARY CATCH WILLIE MAYS
MADE IN THE 1954 WORLD SERIES

"He can play all three outfield positions - at the same time."

LONG-TIME MANAGER GENE MAUCH, ON CESAR CEDENO OF
THE HOUSTON ASTROS

"When I hit a ball, I want someone else to go chase it."

.358 LIFETIME HITTER **ROGERS HORNSBY**, ON GOLF

"In baseball, you hit a home run over the right-field fence, the left-field fence, the center-field fence. Nobody cares. In golf, everything has got to be right over second base."

FORMER BASEBALL PLAYER **KEN HARRELSON**, ON TAKING UP GOLF

"It took me 17 years to get 3,000 hits. I did it in one afternoon on the golf course."

LEGENDARY HALL OF FAMER **HANK AARON**, ON HIS GOLFING ABILITY

"Any game where a man of 60 can beat a man of 30 ain't no game."

LONG-TIME PLAYER AND MANAGER **BURT SHOTTEN**, ON GOLF

"I'm responsible for Joe DiMaggio's success. They never knew how he could go back on a ball until I pitched. All I ever saw of Joe on the field was the back of his uniform. I wouldn't have known what he looked like, except we roomed together."

FELLOW NEW YORK YANKEES HALL OF FAMER
VERNON (LEFTY) GOMEZ

"He has muscles in his hair."

LEFTY GOMEZ, ON HALL OF FAME SLUGGER JIMMIE FOXX

"When Neil Armstrong set foot on the moon, all the scientists were puzzled by an unidentifiable white object. I knew immediately what it was. That was a home run ball hit off me in 1937 by Jimmy Foxx."

LEFTY GOMEZ

"I was so bad I never even broke a bat until last year. Then I was backing out of the garage."

LEFTY GOMEZ, A NOTORIOUSLY POOR-HITTING PITCHER,
ON HIS LACK OF BATTING SKILL

"First triple I ever had."

LEFTY GOMEZ, AFTER BYPASS SURGERY IN 1979

> **"I don't want to throw him nothin'. Maybe he'll just get tired of waitin' and leave."**

LEFTY GOMEZ, WHEN CATCHER
BILL DICKEY ASKED HIM
HOW HE WANTED TO PITCH
TO JIMMY FOXX

"My only day off is the day I pitch."

ROGER CLEMENS, ON HIS LEGENDARY WORKOUT ROUTINE

"One of my chores was to milk the cows, which meant getting up before dawn and going out to that cold, dark barn. I didn't expect to make it all the way to the big leagues; I just had to get away from them damn cows."

CINCINNATI REDS HALL OF FAME OUTFIELDER **EDD ROUSH** (1913 TO 1931), ON WHY HE GOT INTO BASEBALL

"I want to be known as a good major-leaguer, and good major-leaguers work to become good."

SEATTLE MARINER **ALEX RODRIGUEZ**

"He has the best work habits I've ever seen out of a young kid. He takes nothing for granted."

ST. LOUIS CARDINALS HITTING COACH **MITCHELL PAGE**, ON THE CARDINALS' ALBERT PUJOLS

"I got a jackass back in Oklahoma. You can work him from sunup till sundown, and he ain't never gonna win the Kentucky Derby."

ST. LOUIS CARDINAL **PEPPER MARTIN**, WHEN ASKED BY A COACH TO WORK TWICE AS HARD IN PRACTICE

"Every great batter works on the theory that the pitcher is more afraid of him than he is of the pitcher."

DETROIT TIGERS BASEBALL IMMORTAL **TY COBB**

"A pitcher has to look at the hitter as his mortal enemy."

CLEVELAND INDIANS HALL OF FAME PITCHER **EARLY WYNN**

"I don't like to sound egotistical, but every time I stepped up to the plate with a bat in my hands, I couldn't help but feel sorry for the pitcher."

HALL OF FAMER **ROGERS HORNSBY**, WHOSE LIFETIME AVERAGE OF .358 IS SECOND ONLY TO TY COBB

"I always felt the pitcher had the advantage. It's like serving in tennis."

NEW YORK YANKEES PITCHER **ALLIE REYNOLDS**, WHO THREW TWO NO-HITTERS IN 1951

"The pitcher has got only a ball. I've got a bat. So the percentage in weapons is in my favor and I let the fellow with the ball do the fretting."

HALL OF FAMER AND HOME RUN KING **HANK AARON**

"I exploit the greed of all hitters."

MILWAUKEE BRAVES PITCHER **LEW BURDETTE**

"I don't want to give all my little things out. Hitters are pretty stupid, but they do read the papers."

NEW YORK YANKEES PITCHER **RANDY JOHNSON**, DISCUSSING HIS SLIDER WITH NEW YORK TIMES WRITER TYLER KEPNER

"Hitters aren't stupid, but sometimes I think they believe they are smarter than they really are."

ST. LOUIS CARDINALS HALL OF FAME PITCHER **BOB GIBSON**

"Ninety feet between home plate and first base may be the closest man has ever come to perfection."

LEGENDARY SPORTSWRITER RED SMITH

"Baseball is the only sport I know that when you're on offense, the other team controls the ball."

FORMER MAJOR LEAGUER KEN (HAWK) HARRELSON

"When you play this game 20 years, go to bat 10,000 times, and get 3,000 hits, do you know what that means? You've gone 0 for 7,000."

BASEBALL'S ALL-TIME HIT LEADER PETE ROSE, WHO HAD 4,256 HITS IN 14,053 AT-BATS

"One thing about this game: It's really frustrating. In hockey, if your team's losing, you can start a fight. You can get your frustrations out."

LOS ANGELES DODGERS CLOSER ERIC GAGNE

"Baseball is pitching, three-run homers and fundamentals."

BALTIMORE ORIOLES MANAGER EARL WEAVER

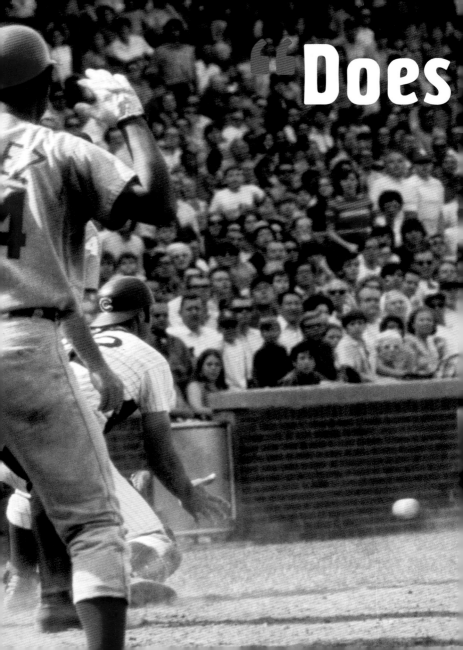

"**Does**

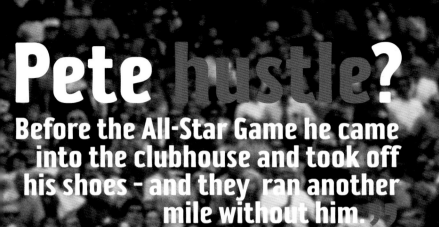

Pete *hustle*?

Before the All-Star Game he came into the clubhouse and took off his shoes – and they ran another mile without him.

HOME RUN KING **HANK AARON**
ON ALL-TIME HIT LEADER PETE (CHARLIE HUSTLE) ROSE

"If you play an aggressive, hustling game, it forces your opponents into errors.... Good Major League teams don't make many mistakes, so by playing aggressively you've got a much better chance to make the error happen."

CINCINNATI REDS STAR **PETE ROSE**

"Run everything out and be in by twelve."

ST. LOUIS CARDINALS MANAGER **RED SCHOENDIENST** TO HIS PLAYERS IN 1968

"As a manager, I ask only one thing of a player – hustle. If a player doesn't hustle, it shows up the club and I show the player up. Hustle is the only thing I demand. It doesn't take any ability to hustle."

NEW YORK YANKEES MANAGER **BILLY MARTIN**

"We tell him,
        'Hey, slow down.
After you touch
    home plate there is
        no other base to
            run to.'"

LOS ANGELES DODGER **RICK MONDAY** ON TEAMMATE
STEVE SAX

"You've gone from Cy Young to Sayonara in one year."

NEW YORK YANKEES THIRD BASEMAN **GRAIG NETTLES**, TO RELIEVER SPARKY LYLE

"Scuse me, somebody important just came in."

NEW YORK RESTAURANT OWNER **TOOTS SHOR**, TO SIR
ALEXANDER FLEMING, DISCOVERER OF PENICILLIN, AFTER
SEEING MEL OTT COME INTO HIS ESTABLISHMENT

"You clowns can go on 'What's My Line?' in full
uniforms and stump the panel."

PITTSBURGH PIRATES MANAGER **BILLY MEYER**, TO HIS
TEAM DURING THEIR 112-LOSS SEASON OF 1952

"This guy is so old that the first time he had
athlete's foot, he used Absorbine Sr."

BROADCASTER **BOB COSTAS**, ON 45-YEAR-OLD PITCHER
TOMMY JOHN

"I know Curt Schilling is happy we got him, because
now Schilling won't have the worst body in the
locker room."

BOSTON RED SOX FIRST BASEMAN **KEVIN MILLAR**, ON THE
TEAM'S ACQUISITION OF DAVID WELLS

"If I had played my career hitting singles like Pete
[Rose], I'd wear a dress."

NEW YORK YANKEES HALL OF FAME SLUGGER
MICKEY MANTLE

"Stubbornness is usually considered a negative, but I think that trait has been a positive for me."

CAL RIPKEN, JR.

"Cal's meant a lot to baseball with his streak. He's been almost like the ambassador for the game."

SEATTLE MARINERS PITCHER RANDY JOHNSON, ON CAL RIPKEN, JR.

"It is extremely impressive that Cal was able to do something like this while playing shortstop. You have to have size and strength, which he obviously has; you have to have skill; and you have to have some luck. I have always thought that shortstops were the best athletes on the field and this just reconfirms that."

ST. LOUIS CARDINALS HALL OF FAME SHORTSTOP OZZIE SMITH, ON CAL RIPKEN, JR.

"Sometimes when he gets hit by a pitch I'm almost embarrassed to ask him about it. By the time he gets back to the dugout the bruise is gone."

ORIOLES TRAINER RICHIE BANCELLS, ON CAL RIPKEN, JR.

"The way to catch a knuckleball is to wait until the ball stops rolling and pick it up."

CATCHER, BROADCASTER AND FUNNYMAN **BOB UECKER**

"It actually giggles at you as it goes by."

LOS ANGELES DODGER **RICK MONDAY**, ON PHIL NIEKRO'S KNUCKLEBALL

"There are two theories on hitting the knuckleball. Unfortunately, neither of them works."

LEGENDARY BATTING INSTRUCTOR **CHARLIE LAU**

"It was great. I got to meet a lot of important people. They all sit behind home plate."

BOB UECKER, ON CATCHING PHIL NIEKRO WITH THE ATLANTA BRAVES IN 1967

"Trying to hit him is like trying to eat Jell-O with chopsticks."

NEW YORK YANKEES OUTFIELDER **BOBBY MURCER**, ON PHIL NIEKRO

"Before Nomo came here, I think everyone looked at Major League Baseball as monsters playing the game. When he came here it showed us we can play the game, too."

SEATTLE MARINER ICHIRO SUZUKI, ON THE DEBT JAPANESE PLAYERS OWE TO PITCHER HIDEO NOMO, WHO WAS THE NATIONAL LEAGUE ROOKIE OF THE YEAR IN 1995

"He's a combination of Michael Jordan and Elvis Presley."

AGENT ARN TELLEM, ON THE POPULARITY OF HIDEKI MATSUI BACK HOME IN JAPAN

"We've had the Chinese team train with the Mariners in the winter. You can see the progress they've made in the last two years. I think at some point China will produce players who can play in the majors. Maybe not in our lifetime, but I think China will produce some players."

PAT GILLICK, WHO SIGNED ICHIRO SUZUKI WHEN HE WAS GENERAL MANAGER OF THE SEATTLE MARINERS

"I see great things in baseball. It's our game – the American game. It will take our people out-of-doors, fill them with oxygen, give them a larger physical stoicism. Tend to relieve us from being a nervous, dyspeptic set. Repair these losses, and be a blessing to us. You could look it up!"

ANNIE SAVOY (SUSAN SARANDON) QUOTING WALT WHITMAN – AND CASEY STENGEL – IN THE MOVIE *BULL DURHAM*

"Correct thinkers think that 'baseball trivia' is an oxymoron: nothing about baseball is trivial."

GEORGE WILL, POLITICAL COMMENTATOR AND AUTHOR OF THE BASEBALL BOOK *MEN AT WORK*

"The romance between intellectuals and the game of baseball is, for the most part, one-sided to the point of absurdity. A large percentage of intelligent Americans evaluate the four hundred men who play major league baseball as awesomely gifted demigods. A large percentage of the muscular four hundred rate intellectuals several notches below umpires."

LEGENDARY BASEBALL WRITER ROGER KAHN

"Luck is the great stabilizer in baseball."

CLEVELAND INDIANS HALL OF FAME PLAYER/MANAGER
TRIS SPEAKER

"Luck is the residue of design."

LEGENDARY BASEBALL EXECUTIVE BRANCH RICKEY

"Bob Gibson is the luckiest pitcher I ever saw. He always pitches when the other team doesn't score any runs."

ST. LOUIS CARDINALS CATCHER TIM MCCARVER,
ON BATTERYMATE BOB GIBSON, WHO WAS 22-9 WITH
A 1.12 ERA IN 1968

"I'm a terrible singer. I feel lucky to play baseball. You can't be gifted in everything."

SEATTLE MARINER ALEX RODRIGUEZ

"There are only two kinds of managers: winning managers and ex-managers."

GIL HODGES, MANAGER OF THE 1969 "MIRACLE METS"

"I'm not the manager because I'm always right, but I'm always right because I'm the manager."

MONTREAL EXPOS MANAGER GENE MAUCH

"The secret of managing a club is to keep the five guys who hate you away from the five guys who are undecided."

NEW YORK YANKEES HALL OF FAME MANAGER
CASEY STENGEL

"The toughest thing for me as a young manager is that a lot of my players saw me play. They know how bad I was."

CHICAGO WHITE SOX MANAGER TONY LARUSSA

"I'm happy for him, that is, if you think becoming a big-league manager is a good thing to have happen to you."

LEGENDARY DODGERS MANAGER WALTER ALSTON, ON
LEARNING THAT FORMER DODGERS PLAYER GIL HODGES
HAD BEEN NAMED MANAGER OF THE NEW YORK METS

"When we lose I can't sleep at night. When we win I can't sleep at night. But when you win you wake up feeling better."

JOE TORRE WHEN MANAGING THE NEW YORK METS

"You can't even celebrate a victory. If you win today, you must start worrying about tomorrow. If you win a pennant, you start worrying about the World Series. As soon as that's over, you start worrying about the next season."

LONGTIME MANAGER BILL MCKECHNIE

"Just hold them for a few innings, fellas. I'll think of something."

BROOKLYN DODGERS MANAGER CHARLIE DRESSEN

"I think we can win it – if my brains hold out."

NEW YORK GIANTS HALL OF FAME MANAGER JOHN MCGRAW,
ON THE 1921 NATIONAL LEAGUE PENNANT RACE (WHICH
THE GIANTS DID WIN)

"I never took the game home with me. I always left it in some bar."

BOB LEMON, A HALL OF FAME PITCHER WHO MANAGED THE
ROYALS, WHITE SOX AND YANKEES BETWEEN 1970 AND 1982

"Why certainly I'd like to have that fellow who hits a home run every time at bat, who strikes out every opposing batter when he's pitching, who throws strikes to any base or the plate when he's playing outfield and who's always thinking about two innings ahead just what he'll do to baffle the other team. Any manager would want a guy like that playing for him. The only trouble is to get him to put down his cup of beer and come down out of the stands and do those things."

PITTSBURGH PIRATES MANAGER DANNY MURTAUGH

"I'm going to Radio Shack to buy one of those head-sets like the broadcasters use. It seems as soon as you put them on, you get 100 times smarter."

PHILADELPHIA PHILLIES MANAGER NICK LEYVA,
ON CRITICISM FROM THE BROADCAST BOOTH

"He should lead the league in everything. With his combination of speed and power he should win the triple batting crown every year. In fact, he should do anything he wants to."

NEW YORK YANKEES MANAGER CASEY STENGEL,
ON A ROOKIE NAMED MICKEY MANTLE

"I wish I was half the ballplayer he is."

DETROIT TIGERS HALL OF FAMER AL KALINE,
ON MICKEY MANTLE

"I always loved the game, but when my legs weren't hurting it was a lot easier to love."

MICKEY MANTLE, ON HIS MANY INJURIES

"On two legs, Mickey Mantle would have been the greatest ballplayer who ever lived."

CHICAGO WHITE SOX HALL OF FAMER NELLIE FOX

"If that guy were healthy, he'd hit 80 home runs."

BOSTON RED SOX HALL OF FAMER CARL YASTRZEMSKI,
ON MICKEY MANTLE

Somebody once asked me if I ever went up to the plate trying to hit a home run. I said, 'Sure, every time.'

MICKEY MANTLE

"What's the matter with you? Other pitchers win their games 9-3, 10-2. You win yours 2-1, 1-0. Why don't you win your games like the others?"

COLONEL JACOB RUPPERT, NEW YORK YANKEES OWNER
FROM 1915 TO 1939, TO STAR PITCHER WAITE HOYT

"We gotta look at that all season!"

CHICAGO CUBS CATCHER GABBY HARNETT, YELLING TO
PLAYERS IN THE AMERICAN LEAGUE DUGOUT AFTER CARL
HUBBELL STRUCK OUT FIVE CONSECUTIVE FUTURE HALL
OF FAMERS DURING THE 1934 ALL-STAR GAME

"If he was throwing the ball any better, we'd have to start a new league for him."

UMPIRE JOHN KIBLER, ON DWIGHT GOODEN DURING
HIS SENSATIONAL 1984 ROOKIE SEASON WITH THE
NEW YORK METS

"Can I throw harder than Joe Wood? Listen mister, no man alive can throw any harder than Smokey Joe Wood."

WASHINGTON SENATORS FLAMETHROWER
WALTER JOHNSON, ON RIVAL PITCHER SMOKEY
JOE WOOD OF THE BOSTON RED SOX

"I threw so hard I thought my arm would fly right off my body."

BOSTON RED SOX PITCHER SMOKEY JOE WOOD, AFTER BEATING THE NEW YORK GIANTS IN GAME ONE OF THE 1912 WORLD SERIES

put a baseball through
a life saver if you asked him.”

HALL OF FAME PLAYER-TURNED-BROADCASTER
JOE MORGAN

"He pitches as though he's double parked."

LEGENDARY DODGERS ANNOUNCER VIN SCULLY,
ON ST. LOUIS CARDINALS GREAT BOB GIBSON

"Trying to hit him was like trying to drink coffee
with a fork."

PITTSBURGH PIRATES HALL OF FAME SLUGGER
WILLIE STARGELL, ON FACING LOS ANGELES DODGERS
STAR SANDY KOUFAX

"Blind people come to the park just to listen to him
pitch."

HALL OF FAME SLUGGER REGGIE JACKSON ON HALL OF
FAME PITCHER TOM SEAVER

"Nothing against Ramiro Mendoza, but this was
Randy Johnson. It's something I can tell my grand-
children about."

BLUE JAYS FIRST BASEMAN ERIC HINSKE (WHO HIT HIS
FIRST CAREER HOME RUN OFF MENDOZA AT YANKEE
STADIUM) ON A TWO-RUN, GAME-WINNING BLAST OFF THE
BIG UNIT

"He must have made that before he died."

NEW YORK YANKEES HALL OF FAMER YOGI BERRA,
AFTER SEEING A STEVE MCQUEEN MOVIE

"A good friend of mine used to say, 'This is a very
simple game. You throw the ball, you catch the ball,
you hit the ball. Sometimes you win, sometimes
you lose, sometimes it rains.' Think about that for a
while."

NUKE LALOOSH (TIM ROBBINS), IN THE MOVIE *BULL DURHAM*

"Quit trying to strike everybody out. Strikeouts are
boring and besides that, they're fascist. Throw
some ground balls. They're more democratic."

CRASH DAVIS (KEVIN COSTNER), TO NUKE LALOOSH
(TIM ROBBINS) IN *BULL DURHAM*

"There are 108 beads in a Catholic rosary. And there
are 108 stitches in a baseball. When I learned that,
I gave Jesus a chance."

ANNIE SAVOY (SUSAN SARANDON), IN *BULL DURHAM*

"There's no crying in baseball."

JIMMY DUGAN (TOM HANKS), IN *A LEAGUE OF THEIR OWN*

"It's supposed to be hard! If it wasn't hard, everyone would do it. The hard is what makes it great!"

JIMMY DUGAN (**TOM HANKS**), TO DOTTIE HINSON (GEENA DAVIS), ON BEING A BASEBALL PLAYER IN THE MOVIE *A LEAGUE OF THEIR OWN*

"He'd give you the shirt off his back. Of course, he'd call a press conference to announce it."

**OAKLAND A'S AND NEW YORK YANKEES TEAMMATE
JIM (CATFISH) HUNTER**, ON REGGIE JACKSON.

"Fans don't **boo** nobodies."

REGGIE JACKSON, WHILE A MEMBER OF THE OAKLAND A'S

"If I played there, they'd name a candy bar after me."

REGGIE JACKSON, ON THE POSSIBILITY OF PLAYING IN NEW YORK

"When you unwrap one, it tells you how good it is."

CATFISH HUNTER, ON THE REGGIE BAR

"I didn't come to New York to be a star. I brought my star with me."

REGGIE JACKSON, ON SIGNING WITH THE YANKEES IN 1977

"October. That's when they pay off for playing ball."

REGGIE JACKSON

"If Ulysses S. Grant had been leading an army of baseball players, they'd have second-guessed him all the way to the doorknob of the Appomattox courthouse."

MAVERICK BASEBALL OWNER BILL VEECK, WHO RAN THE CLEVELAND INDIANS, ST. LOUIS BROWNS AND CHICAGO WHITE SOX BETWEEN 1946 AND 1980

"I get tired of hearing my ballplayers bellyache all the time. They should sit in the pressbox sometimes and watch themselves play."

SAN DIEGO PADRES PRESIDENT BUZZIE BAVASI

"It will revolutionize baseball. It will open a whole new area of alibis for the players."

LONGTIME BASEBALL EXECUTIVE GABE PAUL, ON ARTIFICIAL TURF

"If I ain't startin', I ain't departin'."

ST. LOUIS CARDINALS SHORTSTOP GARY TEMPLETON, ON PLAYING (OR NOT PLAYING) IN THE ALL-STAR GAME

"Do you know what the cardinal sin was on that ball club? To begin a sentence to McGraw with the words 'I thought...' 'You thought?' he would yell. 'With what?'"

HALL OF FAMER **FREDDIE LINSTROM**, ON LEGENDARY NEW YORK GIANTS MANAGER JOHN MCGRAW

"He had an ERA of 3.84 and an IQ to match."

JIM BOUTON, AUTHOR OF THE BASEBALL TELL-ALL BOOK *BALL FOUR*, ON A FELLOW PITCHER

"Out of what? A thousand?"

NEW YORK YANKEES TEAMMATE **MICKEY RIVERS**, AFTER HEARING REGGIE JACKSON BOAST THAT HE HAD AN IQ OF 160

"He can run, hit, throw and field. The only thing Willie Davis has never been able to do is think."

CALIFORNIA ANGELS GENERAL MANAGER **BUZZIE BAVASI**

"There are three types of baseball players: those who make it happen, those who watch it happen, and those who wonder what happened."

LOS ANGELES DODGERS MANAGER **TOMMY LASORDA**

"Good pitching will always stop good hitting and vice versa."

NEW YORK YANKEES HALL OF FAME MANAGER
CASEY STENGEL

"He's dead at the present time."

CASEY STENGEL, REFERRING TO BOSTON BRAVES OUT-
FIELDER LARRY GILBERT, WHO HAD DIED THE YEAR BEFORE

"Best thing wrong with Jack Fisher is nothing."

CASEY STENGEL, ON HIS TOP PITCHER WHEN HE WAS
MANAGING THE NEW YORK METS

"How the hell should I know? Most of the people my age are dead."

CASEY STENGEL, WHEN ASKED WHAT MOST PEOPLE "YOUR
AGE" THINK ABOUT MODERN-DAY BASEBALL

"Mister, that boy couldn't hit the ground if he fell out of an airplane."

CASEY STENGEL, ON A PROSPECT HE SENT TO THE MINORS

"Oldtimers' weekends and airplane landings are alike. If you can walk away from them, they're successful."

CASEY STENGEL

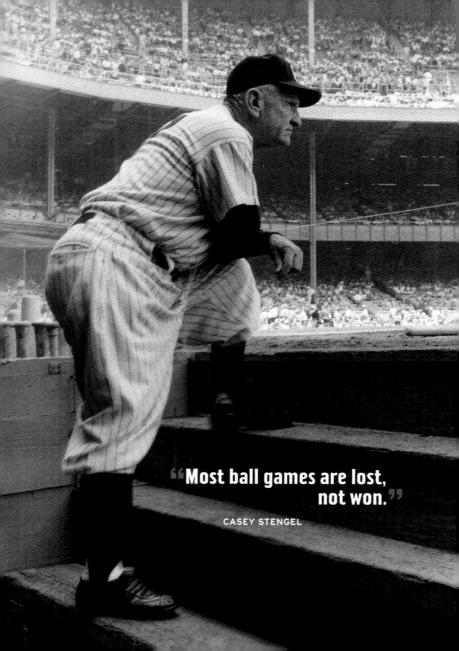

Most ball games are lost, not won.

CASEY STENGEL

"Last year, we had so many people coming in and out they didn't bother to sew their names on the backs of uniforms. They just put them there with Velcro."

PITTSBURGH PIRATES OUTFIELDER **ANDY VAN SLYKE**

"My heart will always be with the Boston fans. I hope that everyone who truly loves me will still support me now that I won't be with the Red Sox."

PEDRO MARTINEZ, ON AGREEING TO TERMS WITH THE NEW YORK METS AFTER THE 2004 SEASON

"I once loved this game. But after being traded four times, I realized that it's nothing but a business. I treat my horses better than the owners treat us."

SLUGGER AND FREE SPIRIT DICK ALLEN, WHO PLAYED ON FIVE DIFFERENT TEAMS IN A 15-YEAR CAREER

"It'll be great not to have to listen to two national anthems."

OUTFIELDER MITCH WEBSTER, ON BEING TRADED TO THE CHICAGO CUBS AFTER PLAYING FOR THE TORONTO BLUE JAYS AND THE MONTREAL EXPOS

"I think that's one of the pluses of being with one club your whole career. People respect the fact that you stayed there through good times and bad."

TONY GWYNN, WHO PLAYED HIS ENTIRE 20-YEAR CAREER WITH THE SAN DIEGO PADRES FROM 1982 TO 2001

"It takes him an hour and a half to watch "60 Minutes"."

HOUSTON ASTROS EXECUTIVE **DONALD DAVIDSON** ON
ASTRO JOE NIEKRO'S ABILITY TO RELAX

"He has the personality of a tree trunk."

NEW YORK METS CATCHER **JOHN STEARNS**, ON TEAMMATE
DAVE KINGMAN

"You know Earl. He's not happy unless he's not happy."

BALTIMORE ORIOLES PLAYER AND COACH
ELROD HENDRICKS ON ORIOLES MANAGER EARL WEAVER

"There isn't enough mustard in the world to cover that hot dog."

OAKLAND A'S PITCHER **DAROLD KNOWLES**, ON TEAMMATE REGGIE JACKSON

"He's not moody, he's just mean. When you're moody, you're sometimes nice."

NEW YORK YANKEES RELIEVER **SPARKY LYLE**, ON YANKEES CATCHER THURMAN MUNSON

"**I'm not sure I know what the hell charisma is, but I get the feeling it's Willie Mays.**"

CINCINNATI REDS FIRST BASEMAN **TED KLUSZEWSKI**

"There is one word in America that says it all, and that one word is 'you never know.'"

PITCHER **JOAQUIN ANDUJAR**, WHO TWICE WON 20 GAMES FOR THE ST. LOUIS CARDINALS

"Trade a player a year too early rather than a year too late."

LEGENDARY BASEBALL EXECUTIVE **BRANCH RICKEY**, LONGTIME GENERAL MANAGER OF THE ST. LOUIS CARDINALS, BROOKLYN DODGERS AND PITTSBURGH PIRATES, AND THE MAN WHO BROUGHT JACKIE ROBINSON TO THE MAJOR LEAGUES

"A man once told me to walk with the Lord. I'd rather walk with the bases loaded."

BALTIMORE ORIOLE **KEN SINGLETON**

"The sun don't shine on the same dog's ass all the time."

HALL OF FAME PITCHER **JIM (CATFISH) HUNTER**, WHO STARRED WITH THE OAKLAND A'S AND NEW YORK YANKEES

"You gotta be careful with your body. Your body is like a bar of soap. The more you use it, the more it wears down."

DICK ALLEN, WHO WAS TRADED FIVE TIMES IN HIS 15-YEAR CAREER

"Close doesn't count in baseball. Close only counts in horseshoes and grenades."

HALL OF FAME SLUGGER FRANK ROBINSON, WHO BECAME THE FIRST BLACK MANAGER IN BASEBALL HISTORY WITH THE CLEVELAND INDIANS IN 1975

"Baseball stuck. Sunday school didn't."

GEORGE WILL, POLITICAL COMMENTATOR AND AUTHOR OF THE BASEBALL BOOK *MEN AT WORK*

"You don't save a pitcher for tomorrow. Tomorrow it may rain."

LEGENDARY MANAGER LEO DUROCHER, WHO MANAGED THE BROOKLYN DODGERS, NEW YORK GIANTS, CHICAGO CUBS AND HOUSTON ASTROS BETWEEN 1939 AND 1973

"A pitcher pitches low instead of high because how often have you seen a 420-foot ground ball?"

HALL OF FAME PITCHER, AND FUTURE U.S. SENATOR FROM KENTUCKY, **JIM BUNNING**

"Pitching is really just an internal struggle between the pitcher and his stuff. If my curve ball is breaking and I'm throwing it where I want, the batter is irrelevant."

BALTIMORE ORIOLES PITCHER **STEVE STONE,**
1980 AMERICAN LEAGUE CY YOUNG AWARD WINNER

"The whole concept is to know what the guy up at bat is looking for but throw it a different speed than he expects."

BALTIMORE ORIOLES PITCHER **MIKE BODDICKER**

"It's the greatest thing in the world when you're a pitcher and you get a hitter looking for one pitch and you throw the other pitch. And you know he was looking for the other pitch, because he never took the bat off his shoulder and it was right down the middle."

NEW YORK YANKEES PITCHER **RANDY JOHNSON**

"He's much more intelligent than I am because he doesn't have a 95 or 98 mile per hour fastball. I would tell any pitcher who wants to be successful to watch him, because he's the true definition of a pitcher."

FIVE-TIME CY YOUNG AWARD WINNER **RANDY JOHNSON**, ON FOUR-TIME CY YOUNG AWARD WINNER GREG MADDUX

"The dumber a pitcher is, the better. When he gets smart and begins to experiment with a lot of different pitches, he's in trouble. All I ever had was a fastball, a curve and a change-up and I did pretty good."

ST. LOUIS CARDINALS HALL OF FAMER **DIZZY DEAN**

Just take the ball and throw it where you want to. Throw strikes.

Home plate don't move."

SATCHEL PAIGE

"Too many pitchers, that's all, there's just too many pitchers. Ten or twelve on a team. Don't see how any of them get enough work. Four starting pitchers and one relief man ought to be enough. Pitch 'em every three days and you'd find they'd get control and good, strong arms."

BASEBALL IMMORTAL **CY YOUNG**, WHO PITCHED FROM 1890 TO 1911, COMMENTING IN 1951

"I could probably throw harder if I wanted, but why? When they're in a jam, a lot of pitchers ... try to throw harder. Me, I try to locate better."

ATLANTA BRAVES PITCHER **GREG MADDUX**

"I throw the ball right down the middle. The high-ball hitters **swing over** it and the low-ball hitters **swing under** it."

PITCHER **SAUL ROGOVIN**, WHO HAD A 48-48 RECORD WITH FOUR DIFFERENT CLUBS DURING HIS EIGHT-YEAR CAREER

"It's a great day for a ballgame; let's play two."

SIGNATURE LINE OF CHICAGO CUBS HALL OF FAMER
ERNIE BANKS

"This kid, right now, the tougher the situation, the more fire he gets in his eyes. You don't teach that."

NEW YORK YANKEES MANAGER JOE TORRE, ON DEREK JETER

"It's not what you did last year. It's what you're going to do this year. That's more important."

ST. LOUIS CARDINALS SLUGGER ALBERT PUJOLS

"The best thing about baseball is that you can do something about yesterday tomorrow."

PHILADELPHIA PHILLIES INFIELDER MANNY TRILLO

"Trust me. I take the field and when the guy says, 'Play ball,' I don't think, 'Okay, I'm going to run into that wall over there and see if I can break my collarbone.' I'm pretty sure I've played my career all out. If I had to run into a wall, I'd do it. Injuries come when you play hard."

OFTEN-INJURED COLORADO ROCKIES SLUGGER
LARRY WALKER

"When I was a small boy in Kansas, a friend of mine and I went fishing and as we sat there in the warmth of the summer afternoon on a river bank, we talked about what we wanted to do when we grew up. I told him I wanted to be a real major league baseball player.... My friend said that he'd like to be president of the United States. Neither of us got our wish."

PRESIDENT DWIGHT D. EISENHOWER

"I know, but I had a better year than Hoover."

NEW YORK YANKEES STAR BABE RUTH, WHOSE $80,000 SALARY IN 1931 WAS MORE THAN THE $75,000 EARNED BY PRESIDENT HERBERT HOOVER

"This is really more fun than being president. I really do love baseball and I wish we could do this out on the lawn every day. I wouldn't even complain if a stray ball came through the Oval Office window now and then."

PRESIDENT RONALD REAGAN, ON PLAYING BASEBALL WITH OLDTIMERS WHILE CELEBRATING NATIONAL BASEBALL MONTH IN 1983

"Hot as Hell, ain't it, Prez?"

BABE RUTH, ON BEING INTRODUCED TO PRESIDENT CALVIN COOLIDGE
ON A WARM DAY AT THE BALLPARK IN WASHINGTON

"Fans, for the past two weeks you have been reading about a bad break. Yet today I consider myself the luckiest man on the face of the earth. I have been in ballparks for 17 years and have never received anything but kindness and encouragement from you fans. Look at these grand men. Which of you wouldn't consider it the highlight of his career just to associate with them for even one day?

OPENING REMARKS MADE BY NEW YORK YANKEES LEGEND LOU GEHRIG ON LOU GEHRIG DAY AT YANKEE STADIUM, JULY 4, 1939. GEHRIG HAD RECENTLY RETIRED AFTER BEING DIAGNOSED WITH AN INCURABLE MUSCLE DISEASE

"I have the greatest job in the world. Only one person can have it. You have shortstops on other teams – I'm not knocking other teams – but there's only one shortstop on the Yankees."

NEW YORK YANKEE DEREK JETER

"It's great to be young and a Yankee."

HALL OF FAMER WAITE HOYT, WHO PITCHED WITH THE YANKEES FROM 1921 TO 1930

"I think the good Lord is a Yankee."

NEW YORK YANKEES RELIEF ACE MARIANO RIVERA

**To play 18 years
in Yankee Stadium is
the best thing that could ever
happen to a ballplayer.**

NEW YORK YANKEES GREAT **MICKEY MANTLE**

"His reputation preceded him before he got here."

NEW YORK YANKEES SLUGGER **DON MATTINGLY**, ON FACING THE METS' DWIGHT GOODEN IN AN EXHIBITION GAME

"Man, it was tough. The wind was blowing about 100 degrees."

TEXAS RANGER MICKEY RIVERS

"Well, that was a cliff-dweller."

NEW YORK METS MANAGER **WES WESTRUM**, AFTER A CLOSE GAME

"I called the doctor and he told me the contraptions were an hour apart."

NEW YORK METS CATCHER **MACKEY SASSER**, ON HOW HE KNEW HIS WIFE HAD GONE INTO LABOR

"It's not a question of morality."

PHILADELPHIA PHILLIES MANAGER **DANNY OZARK**, WHEN ASKED ABOUT HIS TEAM'S MORALE

"O.K., now, everyone inhale and ... dehale."

LOS ANGELES DODGERS SHORTSTOP MAURY WILLS,
LEADING THE TEAM THROUGH CALISTHENICS IN 1962

"Paralyzation due to over-analyzation."

TORONTO TV ANALYST PAT TABLER'S EXPLANATION OF
WHY BLUE JAYS FIRST BASEMAN ERIC HINSKE WAS TAKING
TOO MANY GOOD PITCHES

"Whenever I've pitched, it's been a Samson and Goliath story."

SIX-FOOT-TEN INCH NEW YORK YANKEES RANDY JOHNSON,
MIXING UP BIBLE STORIES

"Me and George and Billy are two of a kind."

MICKEY RIVERS, DENYING HE'D HAVE TROUBLE WITH
GEORGE STEINBRENNER AND BILLY MARTIN IF HE
RETURNED TO THE NEW YORK YANKEES

"Right now, I feel like I've got my feet on the ground
as far as my head is concerned."

SAM BOWEN, A 1974 BOSTON RED SOX DRAFT PICK

"You don't want to be a loser and a winner at the same time, I guess."

SAN DIEGO CATCHER **ROBERT FICK** ON THE POSSIBILITY OF THE 2005 PADRES WINNING THE NL WEST WITH A RECORD BELOW .500

"They're coming out in groves."

BABE RUTH

"You can pitch a gem and lose, but you can't lose when you win."

SAN DIEGO PADRES PITCHER **ERIC SHOW**

"This is the latest I've ever seen nothing not happen."

TORONTO BLUE JAYS GM **J.P. RICCARDI** ON THE LACK OF DEALS BEING MADE AS THE 2005 TRADE DEADLINE APPROACHED

"The penalty is a little more than I expectorated."

BROOKLYN DODGERS OUTFIELDER **FRENCHY BORDAGARY**, AFTER BEING FINED FOR SPITTING AT AN UMPIRE

"It's a beautiful day for a night game."

BROADCASTER AND FORMER MANAGER AND HALL OF FAME PLAYER **FRANKIE FRISCH**

"People ask me what I do in winter when there's no baseball. I'll tell you what I do. I stare out the window and wait for spring."

ROGERS HORNSBY, WHOSE HALL OF FAME CAREER AS A
PLAYER AND MANAGER STRETCHED FROM 1915 TO 1953

"That's the true harbinger of spring, not crocuses or swallows returning to Capistrano, but the sound of a bat on the ball."

BILL VEECK, WHILE OWNER OF THE CHICAGO WHITE SOX
IN 1976

"This is spring training, man, it means you work on things. You don't want to hit .900 in spring training. Spring training stats don't go on the back of your baseball card."

TORONTO BLUE JAY ORLANDO HUDSON

"All winter long, I can't wait for baseball. It gets you back to doing the stuff you love and makes you wish the youthfulness of life could stay with you forever."

TOMMY JOHN, WHO PITCHED FOR SIX TEAMS OVER
26 SEASONS, AND PLAYED UNTIL HE WAS 46 YEARS OLD

"These days baseball is different. You come to spring training, you get your legs ready, your arms loose, your agents ready, your lawyer lined up."

HALL OF FAMER **DAVE WINFIELD** (WHO PLAYED FOR SIX TEAMS IN HIS 22-YEAR CAREER) ON BASEBALL IN THE FREE AGENT ERA

"**Baseball is dull**
only to dull minds."

LEGENDARY SPORTSWRITER **RED SMITH**

"I believe in the Rip van Winkle theory – that a man from 1910 must be able to wake up after being asleep for 70 years, walk into a ballpark and understand baseball perfectly."

BOWIE KUHN, COMMISSIONER OF BASEBALL FROM 1969 TO 1984

"There is still nothing in life as constant and as changing at the same time as an afternoon at a ballpark."

TV PERSONALITY AND COLUMNIST **LARRY KING**

"Baseball's most delicious paradox: although the game never changes, you've never seen everything."

NEW ENGLAND HORRORMEISTER **STEPHEN KING**, WRITING IN THE 2004 RED SOX CHRONICLE *FAITHFUL*

"I can never understand why anybody leaves the game early to beat the traffic. The purpose of baseball is to keep you from caring if you beat the traffic."

KANSAS CITY STAR COLUMNIST **BILL VAUGHAN**

"Any time you think you have the game conquered, the game will turn around and punch you right in the nose."

PHILADELPHIA PHILLIES HALL OF FAMER **MIKE SCHMIDT**, WHO HIT 548 HOME RUNS

"They're like sleeping in a soft bed: easy to get into and hard to get out of."

CINCINNATI REDS HALL OF FAMER **JOHNNY BENCH**, WHO HIT 389 HOME RUNS, ON SLUMPS

"You decide you'll wait for your pitch. Then as the ball starts towards the plate, you think about your stance. And then you think about your swing. And then you realize that the ball that went past you for a strike was your pitch."

NEW YORK YANKEE **BOBBY MURCER**, WHO HIT .277 WITH 252 HOMERS OVER A 17-YEAR CAREER

"When you're hitting the ball, it comes at you looking like a grapefruit. When you're not, it looks like a black-eyed pea."

BOSTON RED SOX SLUGGER **GEORGE SCOTT**, WHO HIT .268 WTH 271 HOMERS OVER A 14-YEAR CAREER

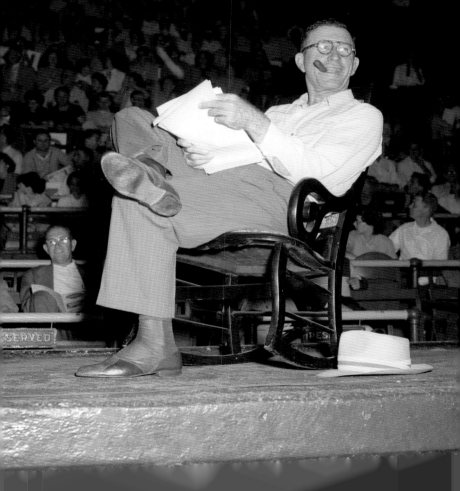

"I have always maintained that the best remedy for a batting slump is two wads of cotton. One in each ear."

MAVERICK BASEBALL OWNER **BILL VEECK**, WHO RAN THE CLEVELAND INDIANS, ST. LOUIS BROWNS AND CHICAGO WHITE SOX BETWEEN 1946 AND 1980

"How in the hell would I know? I haven't caught that pitch yet."

ST. LOUIS CARDINALS CATCHER **BILL DELANCEY**, AFTER BEING ASKED BY MANAGER FRANKIE FRISCH WHAT PITCH GABBY HARNETT HAD JUST HIT FOR A HOME RUN

"Was it difficult to leave the Titanic?"

SAL BANDO, ON HIS DECISION TO LEAVE THE SUCCESSFUL BUT SQUABBLING OAKLAND A'S

"No, why should I?"

NEW YORK YANKEES PITCHER **DON LARSEN**, WHEN ASKED IF HE EVER GOT TIRED OF SPEAKING ABOUT HIS PERFECT GAME IN THE 1956 WORLD SERIES

"I've got to. I can't dance or sing, and we've already got a pitching coach."

LOS ANGELES DODGERS PITCHER **DON SUTTON**, WHEN TOLD TO "HANG IN THERE" BY MANAGER TOMMY LASORDA

"Hey big mouth, how do you spell triple?"

INFAMOUS CHICAGO WHITE SOX STAR SHOELESS JOE JACKSON, AFTER HITTING A THREE-BAGGER, TO A HECKLING FAN WHO KEPT ASKING IF HE COULD SPELL ILLITERATE

"It has to be physical.
That's why I'm soaking my arm now.

If it was **mental,**
I'd be soaking my head."

BOSTON RED SOX PITCHER **JIM LONBORG,** WHO PITCHED ON ONLY
TWO DAYS REST IN THE 1967 WORLD SERIES, WHEN ASKED IF THE
DIFFICULTIES WERE MORE PHYSICAL OR MENTAL

"Why, Mr. Summers, don't you know that the spitter has been outlawed for years? How would I ever learn to throw one?"

DETROIT TIGERS PITCHER **TOMMY BRIDGES** TO UMPIRE BILL SUMMERS AFTER BEING ACCUSED OF THROWING A SPITBALL

"My mother told me never to put my dirty fingers in my mouth."

LOS ANGELES DODGERS HALL OF FAMER **DON DRYSDALE**, DENYING HE EVER THREW A SPITBALL

"I'd always have [grease] in at least two places, in case the umpires would ask me to wipe off one. I never wanted to be caught out here without anything. It wouldn't be professional."

HALL OF FAME PITCHER, AND NOTED SPITBALLER, **GAYLORD PERRY**

"We used to walk up and down the dugout saying, 'Forget about it, hit the dry side.' He'd throw it twice and you'd be looking for it on 116 pitches."

BALTIMORE ORIOLES MANAGER **EARL WEAVER** ON FACING GAYLORD PERRY

"**Not intentionally, but I sweat easy.**"

NEW YORK YANKEES
HALL OF FAMER LEFTY
GOMEZ, WHEN ASKED IF
HE THREW A SPITBALL

"I don't know Jose. I was better than Jose then, and I've been better than him his whole career. If he wants to go make money, go ahead.... For somebody who brags about what he did, I don't see any of your records."

SAN FRANCISCO GIANTS STAR **BARRY BONDS**, ON THE STEROID ALLEGATIONS IN JOSE CANSECO'S BOOK, *JUICED*

"Willie Mays, Hank Aaron, myself, the home run hitters of my time, we were considered big. Now, we'd be midgets."

WASHINGTON NATIONALS MANAGER **FRANK ROBINSON**, WHO WAS SIX-FOOT-ONE AND 195 POUNDS IN HIS PLAYING DAYS AND HIT 586 HOME RUNS

"We're in a competitive business, and these guys were putting up big numbers and helping your ball club win games. You tended to turn your head on things."

SAN DIEGO PADRES GENERAL MANAGER **KEVIN TOWERS**, ADMITTING THAT HE KNEW FOR YEARS ABOUT STEROID USE BY PLAYERS SUCH AS SAN DIEGO'S KEN CAMINITI BUT SAID NOTHING BECAUSE FANS WERE FLOCKING TO SEE THE HOME RUNS

"We didn't know. You have to remember, there was no testing. It was assumed, but nobody could prove it. The concerns with Canseco were more to do with the domestic violence charges than anything with steroids."

GORD ASH, WHO AS GENERAL MANAGER OF THE TORONTO BLUE JAYS SIGNED JOSE CANSECO IN 1998

"Good news. Ten awards have been given out so far, and not one winner has tested positive for steroids."

COMEDIAN CHRIS ROCK, TAKING A SHOT AT BASEBALL WHILE HOSTING THE 2005 ACADEMY AWARDS

"I never took steroids, because I don't need them. The stuff I take, I buy over the counter."

TAMPA BAY DEVIL RAY ALEX SANCHEZ, ADMITTING HE USES MULTIVITAMINS AND ENERGY-BOOSTING MILKSHAKES BUT DENYING HE USES STEROIDS, AFTER BECOMING THE FIRST PLAYER TO FAIL MAJOR LEAGUE BASEBALL'S TEST FOR PERFORMANCE-ENHANCING SUBSTANCES

"Just one. Whenever I hit a home run, I make certain I touch all four bases."

NEW YORK YANKEES STAR **BABE RUTH**, ON SUPERSTITIONS

"Day in and day out, I was consumed by having to do things a certain way. I had 75 to 80 superstitions. They helped me focus in one direction, but it was like a snowball effect. They consume you."

BOSTON RED SOX HALL OF FAMER **WADE BOGGS**, WHO WAS KNOWN AS MUCH FOR ECCENTRICITIES LIKE ALWAYS EATING CHICKEN AS HE WAS FOR HIS FIVE BATTING TITLES AND .328 LIFETIME AVERAGE

"It didn't hurt or help me. I just didn't want to take any chances."

PITTSBURGH PIRATES HALL OF FAMER AND SEVEN-TIME NATIONAL LEAGUE HOME RUN CHAMPION **RALPH KINER**, WHO NEVER STEPPED ON THE FOUL LINE

"I feel every day is different, so whatever I have that day I go with. I don't tie my right shoelace first. I don't do anything like that."

MINNESOTA TWIN AND 2004 CY YOUNG AWARD WINNER
JOHAN SANTANA, DURING A 17-GAME WINNING STREAK
THAT LASTED FROM JULY 11, 2004 TO MAY 1, 2005

"I feel my ability as a ballplayer is over-shadowed by people saying, 'Hey, look at that idiot at the plate.'"

CLEVELAND INDIAN MIKE HARGROVE, WHO WAS NICK-
NAMED "THE HUMAN RAIN DELAY" FOR HIS IDIOSYNCRATIC
MANEUVERS BEFORE STEPPING INTO THE BATTER'S BOX

"Superstitious people don't discuss their superstitions."

RUSTY STAUB, WHO PLAYED 23 MAJOR LEAGUE SEASONS
FOR FIVE DIFFERENT TEAMS (INCLUDING THE NEW YORK
METS AND MONTREAL EXPOS TWICE) FROM 1963 TO 1985

"This losing streak is bad for the fans, no doubt, but look at it this way. We're making a lot of people happy in other cities."

ATLANTA BRAVES OWNER **TED TURNER** FINDS A SILVER LINING DURING A SLUMP

"The fans like to see home runs, and we have assembled a pitching staff for their enjoyment."

MINNESOTA TWINS EXECUTIVE **CLARK GRIFFITH**

"We need just two players to be a contender – Babe Ruth and Sandy Koufax."

TEXAS RANGERS MANAGER **WHITEY HERZOG** IN 1973

"Even Napoleon had his Watergate."

PHILADELPHIA PHILLIES MANAGER **DANNY OZARK**, AFTER A TEN-GAME LOSING STREAK

"Mostly bums."

HALL OF FAMER **ROGERS HORNSBY,** WHEN MANAGING THE BOSTON
BRAVES AND ASKED BY THE OWNER WHAT KIND OF TEAM HE HAD

"They give you a round bat and they throw you a round ball, and then they tell you to hit it square."

PITTSBURGH PIRATES HALL OF FAMER **WILLIE STARGELL**, WHO HIT 475 HOME RUNS

"I've always swung the same way. The difference is when I swing and miss, people say, 'He's swinging for the fences.' But when I swing and make contact people say, 'That's a nice swing.' But there's no difference, it's the same swing."

CHICAGO CUBS SLUGGER **SAMMY SOSA**, THE ONLY PLAYER IN HISTORY WITH THREE 60-HOMER SEASONS

"I swing as hard as I can, and I try to swing right through the ball.... The harder you grip the bat, the more you can swing it through the ball, and the farther the ball will go. I swing big, with everything I've got. I hit big or I miss big. I like to live as big as I can."

NEW YORK YANKEES SLUGGER **BABE RUTH**, WHO HIT 714 HOME RUNS

"I think of myself as 'catching' the ball with my bat and letting the pitcher supply the power."

SAN FRANCISCO GIANTS SLUGGER BARRY BONDS, JUST
THE THIRD PLAYER IN HISTORY TO HIT OVER 700 HOME RUNS

"Hitting is 50 percent above the shoulders."

TED WILLIAMS, AS MANAGER OF THE WASHINGTON
SENATORS. HE HIT .344 WITH 521 HOMERS DURING HIS
CAREER WITH THE BOSTON RED SOX

"Guessing what the pitcher is going to throw is 80 percent of being a successful hitter. The other 20 percent is execution."

HANK AARON, WHO HIT A RECORD 755 HOMERS WITH THE
MILWAUKEE BRAVES, THE ATLANTA BRAVES AND THE
MILWAUKEE BREWERS

"Hitting is an art, but not an exact science."

EIGHT-TIME AMERICAN LEAGUE BATTING CHAMP
ROD CAREW, WHO HIT .328 IN A 19-YEAR CAREER WITH
THE MINNESOTA TWINS AND CALIFORNIA ANGELS

"In the split second from the time the ball leaves the pitcher's hand until it reaches the plate, you have to think about your stride, your hip action, your wrist action; determine how much, if any, the ball is going to break; and then decide whether to swing at it."

BROOKLYN DODGERS HALL OF FAMER DUKE SNIDER, WHO HIT 407 HOMERS, ON WHY HITTING IS HARDER THAN IT LOOKS

"I don't think I can get into my deep inner thoughts about hitting. It's like talking about religion."

PHILADELPHIA PHILLIES HALL OF FAMER MIKE SCHMIDT, WHO LED THE NATIONAL LEAGUE IN HOMERS A RECORD EIGHT TIMES

"Keep your eye on the ball and hit 'em where they ain't."

WEE WILLIE KEELER, WHO HIT .424 FOR THE OLD BALTIMORE ORIOLES IN 1897

"It's the only occupation where a man has to be perfect the first day on the job and then improve over the years."

UMPIRE **ED RUNGE**

"Any umpire who claims he has never missed a play is ... well, an umpire."

UMPIRE **RON LUCIANO**

"How could he be doing his job when he didn't throw me out of the game after the things I called him?"

BALTIMORE ORIOLE **MARK BELANGER** ON UMPIRE RUSS GOETZ

"It seems to me the official rule book should be called the funny pages. It obviously doesn't mean anything. The rule book is only good for you when you go deer hunting and run out of toilet paper."

NEW YORK YANKEES MANAGER **BILLY MARTIN**

"I never questioned the integrity of an umpire. Their eyesight, yes."

LEGENDARY MANAGER **LEO DUROCHER**

"Gentlemen, he was out

because I said he was out."

HALL OF FAME UMPIRE **BILL KLEM**, AFTER BEING SHOWN
PHOTOGRAPHIC EVIDENCE THAT HE HAD BLOWN A CALL

"A concussion of the brain, which many ballplayers might find highly flattering."

> **URBAN SHOCKER** (WHO PITCHED WITH THE NEW YORK YANKEES AND ST. LOUIS BROWNS FROM 1916 TO 1928), DESCRIBING HIS INJURY AFTER BEING HIT IN THE HEAD

"Tests showed there was a brain."

> NEW YORK YANKEES PITCHER **CARL PAVANO**, WHO WAS DIAGNOSED WITH A CONCUSSION AFTER TAKING A LINE DRIVE OFF HIS HEAD EARLY IN THE 2005 SEASON

"No more than usual."

> PITTSBURGH PIRATES SLUGGER AND NOTORIOUSLY POOR FIELDER **DICK STUART**, WHEN ASKED IF HE WAS DIZZY AFTER BEING HIT IN THE HEAD WITH A PITCH

"I took the two most expensive aspirins in history."

> NEW YORK YANKEE **WALLY PIPP**, ON THE HEADACHE THAT TOOK HIM OUT OF THE LINEUP AND LAUNCHED LOU GEHRIG'S STREAK OF 2,130 CONSECUTIVE GAMES PLAYED

"The doctors X-rayed my head and found nothing."

ST. LOUIS CARDINALS HALL OF FAMER **DIZZY DEAN**, AFTER TAKING A THROW IN THE HEAD DURING THE 1934 WORLD' SERIES

❝Touch 'em all Joe.
You'll never hit a bigger home run in your life!❞

TORONTO BLUE JAYS BROADCASTER **TOM CHEEK**, CALLING
JOE CARTER'S THREE-RUN HOMER IN THE BOTTOM OF THE
NINTH THAT DEFEATED THE PHILADELPHIA PHILLIES IN THE
1993 WORLD SERIES

"They say you should swing hard in case you make
contact, and that's pretty much what I was doing.
And I was going to score whether I had to straight-
arm somebody or step on them, or whatever. This
is a great crowd and I knew they would go sky
high and swarm out onto the field. I made sure to
touch everything that was white. I didn't want to
miss a base."

BOSTON RED SOX CATCHER **CARLTON FISK**, AFTER HIS
12TH-INNING HOME RUN TO WIN GAME SIX OF THE 1975
WORLD SERIES

"It's like the Kennedy assassination. Everyone I see comes up and tells me where they were and what they were doing when Gibson hit that home run."

OAKLAND A'S RELIEF ACE **DENNIS ECKERSLEY**, ON THE PINCH-HIT HOMER AN INJURED KIRK GIBSON HIT OFF HIM IN GAME ONE OF THE 1988 WORLD SERIES

"Go crazy, folks! Go crazy!"

ST. LOUIS CARDINALS BROADCASTER **JACK BUCK** CALLING THE SHOCKING GAME-WINNING HOMER BY LIGHT-HITTING DEFENSIVE WIZARD OZZIE SMITH IN THE BOTTOM OF THE NINTH AGAINST THE LOS ANGELES DODGERS IN GAME FIVE OF THE 1985 NATIONAL LEAGUE CHAMPIONSHIP SERIES

"The last time I hit a home run in the bottom of the ninth to win the game was in Strat-O-Matic."

NEW YORK MET **LENNY DYKSTRA**, ON HOMERING TO BEAT THE HOUSTON ASTROS IN GAME THREE OF THE 1986 NATIONAL LEAGUE CHAMPIONSHIP SERIES

"THERE'S A LONG DRIVE! THAT'S GONNA BE IT, I BELIEVE! THE GIANTS WIN THE PENNANT!! THE GIANTS WIN THE PENNANT!! THE GIANTS WIN THE PENNANT!! THE GIANTS WIN THE PENNANT!! BOBBY THOMSON HITS INTO THE LOWER DECK OF THE LEFT-FIELD STANDS! THE GIANTS WIN THE PENNANT, AND THEY'RE GOING CRAZY! THEY'RE GOING CRAZY!"

RUSS HODGES' CALL OF BOBBY THOMPSON'S GAME-WINNING HOMER IN THE BOTTOM OF THE NINTH TO GIVE THE GIANTS THE 1951 NATIONAL LEAGUE PENNANT IN THE FINAL GAME OF THEIR BEST-OF-THREE PLAYOFF WITH THE BROOKLYN DODGERS

"**Why pitch nine innings when you can get just as famous pitching two?**"

NEW YORK YANKEES RELIEF ACE **SPARKY LYLE**

"The two most important things in life are good friends and a strong bullpen."

BOB LEMON, A HALL OF FAME PITCHER WHO LATER
MANAGED THE ROYALS, WHITE SOX AND YANKEES
BETWEEN 1970 AND 1982

"You just listen to the ball and bat come together. They make an awful noise."

BOSTON RED SOX MANAGER **DARRELL JOHNSON**, ON WHEN
TO CHANGE PITCHERS

"I call Mo 'the Equalizer.' I mean, I can't tell you how comforting it felt to have him come in when I left the game."

NEW YORK YANKEES PITCHER **ROGER CLEMENS**

"It's the best feeling in the world. The game's on the line, and you're the guy in the spotlight."

LOS ANGELES DODGERS CLOSER **ERIC GAGNE**

"I told him I wasn't tired. He told me, 'No, but the outfielders sure are."

TEXAS RANGERS RELIEVER **JIM KERN**, ON WHAT THE MAN-
AGER SAID WHEN TAKING HIM OUT OF A GAME

"Whoever answers the bullpen phone."

TEXAS RANGERS PITCHING COACH **CHUCK ESTRADA**, ON
HOW HE DECIDES WHICH RELIEVER TO USE ON HIS LAST-
PLACE TEAM

"I want to thank all the pitchers who couldn't go
nine innings, and manager Dick Howser, who
wouldn't let them."

KANSAS CITY ROYALS RELIEF ACE **DAN QUISENBERRY**, ON
WINNING THE 1982 AMERICAN LEAGUE FIREMAN OF THE
YEAR AWARD

"He can't hit, he can't run, he can't field, he can't throw.

He can't do a goddamn thing but beat you. "

BROOKLYN DODGERS GM **BRANCH RICKEY** ON EDDIE STANKY

"You play the game to win the game, and not to worry about what's on the back of the baseball card at the end of the year."

NEW YORK YANKEE **PAUL O'NEILL**, ON THE TEAM OF THE LATE 1990s AND EARLY 2000s

"If a guy went o-for-8 and we won a doubleheader, I'd expect this guy to be happy, right? And say we lost a doubleheader and he goes 7-for-8 and he's joking around the clubhouse – forget those guys. I don't want him to be laughing when we're losing and he gets his hits. To me, that's an individual-type ballplayer."

NEW YORK YANKEE **MOOSE SKOWRON**, ON THE TEAM OF THE LATE 1950s AND EARLY 1960s

"My dad would have bopped me on the head when I was a kid if I came home bragging about what I did on the field. He only wanted to know what the team did."

KEN GRIFFEY, JR. ON HIS FATHER, KEN GRIFFEY, SR.

"And if I have my choice between a pennant and a triple crown, I'll take the pennant every time."

BOSTON RED SOX STAR **CARL YASTRZEMSKI**, WHO WON BOTH IN 1967

"If you're going to play at all, you're out to win. Baseball, board games, playing Jeopardy, I hate to lose."

NEW YORK YANKEES STAR **DEREK JETER**

"When you work for George Steinbrenner, whether you're the favorite or you're not the favorite, you're expected to win."

NEW YORK YANKEES MANAGER **JOE TORRE**

"If I were playing third base and my mother were rounding third with the run that was going to beat us, I'd trip her. Oh, I'd pick her up and brush her off and say, 'Sorry, Mom,' but nobody beats me."

LEGENDARY MANAGER (AND SCRAPPY EX-PLAYER)
LEO DUROCHER

"Grantland Rice, the great sportswriter, once said, 'It's not whether you win or lose, it's how you play the game.' Well Grantland Rice can go to hell, as far as I'm concerned."

LONGTIME CALIFORNIA ANGELS OWNER (AND FORMER
SINGING COWBOY) GENE AUTRY

"You have to bear in mind that Mr. Autry's favorite horse was named Champion. He ain't ever had one called Runner-Up."

CALIFORNIA ANGELS MANAGER GENE MAUCH,
ON THE CLUB OWNER

"On my tombstone, just write: 'The sorest loser that ever lived.'"

BALTIMORE ORIOLES MANAGER EARL WEAVER

"I don't want to mellow. I'd rather be known as a winner and a poor loser."

BOSTON RED SOX MANAGER DICK WILLIAMS

"I need to win, man. I've had numbers, but I've never won a World Series."

SAN FRANCISCO GIANTS SUPERSTAR BARRY BONDS

"I don't know nothin' about nothin', I'm just glad we won."

BLUE JAYS PITCHER JIM ACKER, WHEN ASKED FOR HIS THOUGHTS AFTER TORONTO WON THE AMERICAN LEAGUE EAST IN 1985

"So I'm ugly. So what? I never saw anyone hit with his face."

YOGI BERRA

"We have deep depth."

NEW YORK YANKEES HALL OF FAME CATCHER YOGI BERRA

"You can't think and hit at the same time."

YOGI BERRA

"A nickel ain't worth a dime anymore."

YOGI BERRA

"Bill Dickey learned me all his experiences."

YOGI BERRA

"I don't know. I'm not in shape yet."

YOGI BERRA, WHEN ASKED HIS CAP SIZE

"I want to thank you for making this day necessary."

YOGI BERRA, ON BEING HONORED BY THE FANS IN HIS
HOMETOWN OF ST. LOUIS

"If the people don't want to come out to the park,
nobody's going to stop them."

YOGI BERRA, ON ATTENDANCE WOES IN KANSAS CITY

"It's so crowded nobody goes there anymore."

YOGI BERRA, ON TOOTS SHOR'S RESTAURANT

"I knew I was going to take the wrong train, so I left
early."

YOGI BERRA

"Our similarities are different."

DALE BERRA, COMPARING HIMSELF TO HIS FAMOUS
FATHER YOGI

cover: Elsa/Getty Images; title page: Ezra Shaw/Getty Images; 8 New York Times Company/Getty Images; 15 John Dominis/Time Life Pictures/Getty Images; 19tl National Baseball Hall of Fame/MLB Photos/Getty Images; 19tr Jed Jacobson/Getty Images; 19m Michael Zagaris/MLB Photos/Getty Images; 19bl Focus on Sport/Getty Images; 19br Photo File/MLB Photos/Getty Images; 21 AP Photo; 26 Colin Braley/Reuters; 29 Jim McIsaac/Getty Images; 32 National Baseball Hall of Fame/MLB Photos/Getty Images; 37 Bettman/Corbis 39 Jed Jacobson/Getty Images; 43,49 National Baseball Hall of Fame/MLB Photos/Getty Images; 57 Nick Laham/Getty Images; 61 National Baseball Hall of Fame/MLB Photos/Getty Images; 62 Doug Pensinger/Getty Images; 68 Focus on Sport/Getty Images; 75 AFP/Getty Images; 80 Focus on Sport/Getty Images; 83 Otto Gruele Jr./Getty Images; 87 Photo File/MLB Photos/Getty Images; 88 MLB Photos/Getty Images; 91 Bruce Bennett Studios/Getty Images; 92 Chris Trotman/Getty Images; 99 Arnold Newman/Getty Images; 104 Bettman/Corbis; 108 Diamond Images/Getty Images; 111 George Silk/Time Life Pictures/Getty Images; 117,121 Rich Pilling/MLB Photos/Getty Images 123 Jim McIsaac/Getty Images; 124 National Baseball Hall of Fame/MLB Photos/Getty Images; 131, 137, 143 Bettman/Corbis; 145, 148r Jonathan Daniel/Getty Images; 148tl Ralph Morse/Time Life Pictures/Getty Images; 148bl Rich Pilling/MLB Photos/Getty Images; 155 Rick Stewart/Allsport/Getty Images; 158 AP Photo; 169 Photo File/Getty Images

Eric Zweig is an author, editor and sports historian. His articles have appeared in numerous publications including the *Toronto Star*, the *Globe and Mail* and the *Toronto Sun*. He is the author or editor of dozens of books including *Total Hockey, 99: My Life in Pictures* and *The Toronto Blue Jays Official 25th Anniversary Commemorative Book*. A former member of the Toronto Blue Jays grounds crew, he still has a champagne bottle from the club's first American League East Division title celebration in 1985.

Bruce County Public Library
1243 Mackenzie Rd.
Port Elgin ON N0H 2C6